THE RAW DEAL

THE RAW DEAL

How Myths and Misinformation
about Deficits, Inflation, and
Wealth Impoverish America

ELLEN FRANK

BEACON PRESS

BOSTON

BEACON PRESS
25 Beacon Street
Boston, Massachusetts 02108-2892
www.beacon.org

Beacon Press books
are published under the auspices of
the Unitarian Universalist Association of Congregations.

07 06 05 04   8 7 6 5 4 3 2 1

This book is printed on acid-free paper that meets the uncoated paper
ANSI/NISO specifications for permanence as revised in 1992.

Text design by Isaac Tobin
Composition by Wilsted & Taylor Publishing Services

LIBRARY OF CONGRESS CATALOGING-IN-PUBLICATION DATA

Frank, Ellen.
   The raw deal : how myths and misinformation about deficits,
inflation, and wealth impoverish America / Ellen Frank.
      p. cm.
   Includes bibliographical references and index.
   ISBN 0-8070-4726-0 (cloth : alk. paper)
    1. Money—United States. 2. Deficits—United States. 3. Inflation
(Finance)—United States. 4. Wealth—United States. 5. Social
justice—United States. I. Title.

HG540.F73 2004
330.973—dc22   2003025982

CONTENTS

CHAPTER ONE

INTRODUCTION

In 2001 the National Bureau of Economic Research published an exhaustive study documenting what economists and government statisticians had long suspected. From 1980 to 1998 most of the benefits of economic growth in the United States flowed to the very wealthiest families. Although the U.S. economy grew, average wages fell during the 1980s and through much of the 1990s. Middle-income families maintained their living standards—barely—and only because women worked more hours outside the home. Yet the most affluent 1 percent of families nearly tripled their incomes—to an average $515,000. Most of this ended up in the hands of the richest thirteen thousand families, whose earnings by 1998 averaged $17 million.[1] U.S. income had not been concentrated in so few hands since the 1920s.

Corporate scandals in 2002 provided the public with a rare glimpse into the lifestyles of some of these thirteen thousand families—corporate titans of astounding wealth and their fantastically remunerated confidants on Wall Street. *Business Week* estimated that by 2002, the typical CEO of a major U.S. corporation earned $37 million, four and a half times what they had earned in 1989 and a thousand times as much as the typical American worker.

Incomes this large cannot possibly be spent, but are mostly saved and held in financial assets like stocks and bonds. So it is little surprise that as the nation's income flowed into fewer and fewer hands, financial wealth became concentrated as well. Surveys of wealth distribution conducted every few years by the Federal Reserve found the rich growing immensely richer during the 1980s and 1990s. By 1998, the richest 1 percent of U.S. households controlled half of all financial assets.

With wealth comes the ability to command even more income and amass still greater wealth. During the 1980s and 1990s, capital income—income derived from ownership of assets rather than from work—rose to levels last seen in the late 1920s. Numerous commentators called the 1990s a new Gilded Age. The political analyst Kevin Phillips worried that the United States was fast becoming a "plutocracy" in which wealth would "reach beyond its own realm of money and control politics and government as well."[2]

How the rich in the United States captured such astonishing gains is a long and complicated tale. The story begins in the 1970s with jobs moving first to the nonunion South, then to Mexico and overseas, leaving behind shuttered factories and weakened unions. It continues with the mounting influence of wealth on the political system—campaign funding, lobbying efforts, think tanks, foundations, and cushy sinecures for former political officials. These stories have been amply documented elsewhere and are, in any case, depressingly evident to a diligent reader of any major daily or news magazine.³

But the story of the decline of the middle class and rise of the plutocrats is also an account of battles over inflation in the late 1970s that ended when interest rates tripled in 1981 and financial investors pressured corporations to generate comparable returns on stocks. It is a story of the triumph of the finance industry—the banks, brokers, deal makers, and their clients—and the growing dominance of financial interests both in setting U.S. economic policy and in setting limits on public discourse about U.S. economic policy. That is the subject of this book.

MONEY ILLUSION

In money-driven, market economies, people naturally conceive the economy in terms of money, numbers, dollars and cents, so much so that they often lose sight of the intrinsic value of things. Economists term the tendency to equate monetary with real improvements in well-being "money illusion." Money becomes a veil that confuses and distorts our perception of our true interests. In recent years, American political discourse has exhibited a deep and virulent form of money illusion that has been propagated by conservative and financial interests and whose primary function has been to protect the power and perquisites of wealth.

Financial wealth, after all, consists of nothing more than bits of paper and entries in computer databases—stocks, bonds, bank accounts, brokerage and trust fund balances—

3

signifying legal claims to real resources. Money itself is simply more paper, paper that a government prints and can control. How governments control money determines how much real economic power attaches to financial wealth.

Governments, for example, can print money and put it into the hands of those without it. They can drive down interest rates and reduce the incomes earned on financial assets. They can dictate the terms and conditions under which money can leave the country and the rate at which it can be exchanged for other currencies. Governments not only can do these things, they do them routinely. These are aspects of monetary policy and every modern economy possesses the institutions and proficiency to carry them out.

Contemporary governments possess still more powerful tools to regulate the prerogatives of wealth. They can borrow private wealth and divert it to public purposes. A national government's capacity to borrow and print money enables it to regulate critical economic services—health care and education, for example—and distribute them free of charge to all citizens. In this way governments diminish the economic power associated with wealth, since wealth is no longer the sole criterion for determining who gets access to resources. These are aspects of fiscal and social welfare policy and have long been part of the policy repertoire of developed economies.

So why—after nearly twenty-five years of stagnant wages, less secure jobs, and longer working hours, after financial scandals exposed the phenomenal wealth and lavish spending of the very rich—does the American public not clamor

for its elected officials to redistribute wealth or at least to di-
lute its power?

A major reason, this book argues, is that since the 1980s
the rhetoric of economic policy in the United States has become so convoluted and confusing, so entangled in mystifi-
cation and obfuscation, that it requires an entire book to
unravel the mythologies and illusions surrounding finance,
money, debt, and economics and set the record straight.

So confounding have economic policy debates become in
recent years that ordinary wage and salary earners find it
difficult to protect their economic interests or even to fully
comprehend where those interests lie. In the United States
today, people are told that economic growth cannot proceed
unless Americans save more, but that the world economy
depends on the free-spending American consumer. They
are told that any cutback in consumer borrowing will plunge
the economy into recession, but that Americans borrow
irresponsibly and need the discipline of more punitive
bankruptcy laws. They are told that their taxes are being put
aside for their old age, but that federal old-age programs will
be bankrupt when they retire. Americans are told to save
their own way out of economic difficulties and invest their
savings in stocks, but warned that secure jobs hurt profits
and make those stocks fall in value. They are told that government borrowing will burden them with debt and that repaying the debt will lower interest rates, but that low interest
rates cause inflation and inflation will ruin them.

Contradictory economic rhetoric serves two political
goals. First, half-baked but seductive arguments about fi-

nance enlist the general public in support of policies—like tax breaks for stock investing, restrictive monetary policy, federal and international debt repayment—mostly harmful to the public, but beneficial to those with considerable wealth. Second, obscure and confusing economic arguments about finance and money foreclose discussion or even consideration of policies that might generate a more egalitarian distribution of the economy's output. Artificial financial and accounting obstacles—the need to balance budgets or encourage saving or preempt inflation—are invoked to preclude debate about collective responses to major life challenges like illness, child rearing, and aging, leaving individuals with few realistic or even comprehensible options but to fend for themselves.

In the United States, financial illusions infect both politics and popular culture. Until the stock market stalled in 2000, news commentators encouraged Americans to aspire to instant wealth in the financial markets by highlighting the relatively rare cases of extraordinary financial success while downplaying the more common experience of financial difficulty. Media commentators and political spokesmen failed to note the corrosive affects a rising stock market could have on the prospects of average households—ignoring the fact, for example, that stock gains all too often followed announcements of corporate layoffs and restructuring.

Throughout the 1990s, media and political figures alike applauded the Federal Reserve's inflation-fighting hikes in interest rates. Few mentioned that the Fed's clear intent was to slow growth in the U.S. economy. The strong dollar was lauded as a symbol of U.S. power and prosperity; the strain it placed on workers in export industries here and on indebted countries abroad merited little remark. The federal government's growing budget surplus garnered universally favorable comment, as if the government's accumulating tax dollars was akin to a family's accumulating wealth. Virtually no one noted that federal surpluses, by taking spending power out of the economy, can wreak economic havoc. Nor did the federal government's continual fiscal retrenchment—cuts in welfare, in Medicare and Medicaid, and spending caps on virtually all "discretionary" programs—elicit much concern. Who, after all, needs government programs when the stock market will make you fabulously wealthy?

Culturally, the power of financial rhetoric rests on the unarticulated premise that individual economic prospects are unbounded, that individual success is not tethered to the success of the economy as a whole. The language of savings and finance engenders a retrograde, solipsistic understanding of how the economy works, a distorted worldview of extreme individualism and self-reliance that ignores the innumerable interdependencies of economic life. Money provides the illusion that its possessor is independent and self-sufficient.

THE REAL ECONOMY

But we are not self-sufficient. Though we experience the economy as individuals—earning our own keep, watching our own portfolios—economic life is fundamentally social and reciprocal. Ultimately we survive on actual goods and services—food, clothing, childcare, housing—which are produced cooperatively and shared among the population. Growth in the real, productive economy—the amount of goods and services available each year—places an absolute limit on how much there is to go around. No amount of saving, financial planning, or paper wealth generated in the markets can alter this equation.

Simple arithmetic dictates that the average standard of living in a society cannot grow faster than that society's output. Therefore, no one person's share can grow by more than the average unless somebody, somewhere, gets stuck with a smaller slice of the economic pie. If the economy grows at, say, 4 percent per year, then there will be only 4 percent more stuff—cars, bread, haircuts, housing—to go around. Some people, through luck or clever financial transactions, might manage to increase their own incomes by more than 4 percent. But when a lucky few investment specialists or CEOs realize tremendous gains, it stands to reason that others somewhere down the line either suffer losses or receive less than a full share of the economy's growth.

For most Americans, the key to prosperity lies in the steady expansion of the real economy—the production of actual goods and services. If this economy functions smoothly, if production grows as rapidly as the population, with perhaps some additional growth as workers become more productive, then the real economy will make possible a stable or slowly rising standard of living for all. Whether economic growth actually benefits the majority depends on three factors.

First, the economy must grow smoothly and dependably without periodic crashes and recessions. Second, it must generate enough jobs to employ all those willing and able to work. Growth without employment means falling wages and greater inequality. Third, because market economies often fail on counts one and two, societies must develop institutions to indemnify people against unemployment, aging, and misfortune and to disperse the benefits of growth widely. These include social insurance programs like unemployment compensation and Social Security as well as public services—libraries, schools, and so forth—that make minimal amenities available to all. When such institutions are in place, a country's real wealth will be shared—even if its money wealth is not—and the majority of people will thrive.

Only for the already rich is prosperity tied to the growth of the money economy—the endlessly and exhaustingly chronicled sphere of brokering, trading, lending, and borrowing that transfixes the business press. In this economy, people trade stocks and currencies, make deals, manage portfolios, and buy and sell companies. Fortunes are hedged, leveraged, invested, and fabulously compounded. Because financial wealth is concentrated in so few hands, gains in the financial economy tend also to be concentrated and policies designed to benefit the finance sector rarely protect the material interests of the majority.

Yet during the 1980s and 1990s, every oscillation in the

Dow or the NASDAQ was breathlessly recorded, filling the business section of each daily paper, headlining the economic news of CNN and MSNBC and peppering the speeches of political candidates. This sphere of venture capitalists and Wall Street whizzes made many people astonishingly wealthy, and ordinary Americans were encouraged to turn away from material concerns and become financiers themselves.

In this, the 1980s and 1990s represented a distinct break from postwar economic history. After World War II, financial markets were sluggish and boring. The Dow Jones Industrial Average of stock prices inched up from 600 in 1960 to just under 900 twenty years later. This works out to an average annual return of less than 2 percent—when dividends are added in, a bit more than one could have earned in a plain vanilla savings account. Returns available on other financial assets like bonds and bank accounts were regulated by the Federal Reserve until the late 1970s and remained relatively low until the 1980s. It was hard to get rich from finance.

But it was hardly necessary to dabble at high finance in order to improve one's economic position. As subsequent chapters will explain, numerous institutions had been set up after the war to promote economic growth and employment both nationally and internationally. In the developed economies, ordinary people flourished through work and production. Thanks to low unemployment rates and rapid growth in the productivity of the real economy, U.S. families at all socioeconomic levels—rich, poor, and middle class—doubled their incomes between 1945 and 1975. Both incomes and ownership of wealth grew more equitable, as middle-class families acquired homes, cars, and other assets. The share of wealth held by the richest 1 percent of families declined from 30 percent in 1940 to 20 percent in 1970.

Change began in the late 1970s. Incomes earned through regular work fell slowly but steadily for employees of all sorts—skilled, unskilled, educated, uneducated. At the same time, interest rates, stock prices, and executive pay packages soared. By 1998, the richest 1 percent garnered as much income as the lowest-earning 40 percent of American families.

Contrast the fortunes of a wage earner to those of a stock market investor in the 1980s and 1990s. Someone who bought $1,000 worth of stocks in major corporations in 1981 could have sold them in 2000 for $10,600—a whopping average annual return of 13 percent before dividends, far more than one could have earned in almost any other endeavor. Interest rates spiked in the early 1980s and, after adjusting for inflation, remained high over much of the next twenty years. Income flowed to the financial markets and investors clamored for continued high returns year after year, transforming the management of U.S corporations.

Robert Frank and Philip Cook describe the contemporary U.S. economy as a "winner-take-all society" in which a few lucky, shrewd, or well-placed individuals reap huge rewards while earnings for the vast majority stagnate.[4] During the 1980s and 1990s, the financial world, with its soaring stock prices, instantaneous gains, and astonishing returns was the world of the economic winners.

Yet the financial world produces little of actual material value. Although hundreds of trillions of dollars pass through it each year, the entire finance industry generates only about 3 percent of U.S. output and employment. Most financial transactions entail little more than shifting ownership of stocks, bonds, and deeds to property from hand to hand. As shown in the following chapters, unregulated financial deal-making, though helpful in moving money and credit through the economy, often serves to concentrate wealth and can be immensely disruptive to the productive economy. Moreover, the rhetoric of finance and the politics financial interests inspire are profoundly at odds with the economic interests of those whose livelihoods lie in the workaday economy.

THE RAW DEAL

As real economic issues have become hopelessly ensnarled in financial jargon, ordinary citizens receive an increasingly raw deal from their governments. Political solutions to economic insecurities are ruled out, not because they are unworkable or unwanted by voters, but because they fail to satisfy irrelevant financial criteria—like the need for a balanced budget. Since the 1980s, the administrations of Presidents Ronald Reagan, George H. W. Bush, Bill Clinton, and George W. Bush have strategically exploited public ignorance of economics, cynically misrepresenting the nature of government finances and presenting accounting conventions as absolute barriers that could not be breached, not even to address unemployment or other pressing social needs.

As chapter 3 will detail, economists, political consultants, and speechwriters in the United States and abroad have fashioned a parable that casts national governments as ordinary households, afflicted by the same economic anxieties and constraints and hampered by the same need to placate creditors and exercise financial prudence.

The gradual but relentless effort to cut government programs established during the New Deal has dampened public expectations of any political response to individual economic distress. Today, few Americans have reason to expect, despite repeated assurances by elected officials to the contrary, that public policy will address their health, education, housing, employment, and retirement concerns. Proposed health care reform measures languish or, like the 2003 Medicare prescription drug benefit legislation, prove disappointing and inadequate. Aids to the unemployed are cut as are funds allocated for education. Politicians and the media provide confusing and contradictory accounts of the status of Social Security and Medicare. Faced with deteriorating social supports, more and more people understandably turn their attention to shoring up their individual finances.

Under the thrall of financial illusions, Americans are encouraged to partake in the spectacular riches being created on Wall Street, rather than demanding a better deal from their government. Employers switch from old-fashioned pension plans to newly fashionable personal retirement accounts, in the process shifting the financial risks of retirement onto their employees. In the 1990s the Clinton administration proposed federally sponsored individual investment accounts to partially replace Social Security, conducting detailed planning of how such accounts would work. In 2002 a presidential commission appointed by the Bush administration recommended that Social Security funds be diverted to individual investment accounts and invested in the stock market.[5] Despite the collapse in the early 2000s of technology and energy firms, whose bankruptcy exposed the vulnerability of personal retirement accounts, U.S. corporations continue to eliminate traditional pension and health plans, leaving Americans increasingly reliant on personal savings to fund retirement, health, and education.

During the closing decades of the twentieth century, both Democrats and Republicans seemed to agree that every social problem or economic difficulty—meeting rising health care costs, paying for college education, saving for retirement, providing care for dependents—could be solved with some sort of tax-exempt savings plan or financial insurance scheme. And why not? With returns on stocks soaring and inflation-adjusted interest on bonds at historic highs during much of the 1980s and 1990s, financial investing certainly seemed the cure for any number of ills.

Financial firms—mutual funds, insurance companies, investment houses—were among the most profitable businesses in the country. Toss money to them and it came back miraculously enlarged, compounded, and multiplied. Public schools introduced stock market games to teach junior high students lessons in both math and civics.[6] The liberal

Urban League bemoaned the lack of financial savvy among inner-city minorities and sponsored financial-management classes and investment clubs.[7]

The economic changes of the late twentieth century brought an unprecedented upsurge in lottery participation, casino gambling, and small-scale stock trading as individuals sought to become the winners, not the losers. But for every lottery winner, there are thousands and thousands of losers, each out a few bucks. What's more, much as each individual may convince herself that she, not others, will win, the likely distribution of winners and losers in a finance-driven, winner-take-all economy is depressingly predictable. Just as lotteries benefit the states that run them and slot machines enrich the operators of casinos, gains in the world of finance accrue primarily to those already holding the cards—the already wealthy, as chapter 2 explains. The occasional rags-to-riches success story does not invalidate this any more than the occasional blackjack winner means that casinos are not immensely profitable to their owners. As the stock market soared, financial gains flowed disproportionately to the relatively small number of households that started out with substantial wealth or an inside track.

Meanwhile, wealthy conservatives and corporations shower funds on conservative think tanks and policy institutes—the Cato and American Enterprise Institutes, the Heritage and Olin Foundations—which have became a source of ceaseless antigovernment, promarket, finance-driven rhetoric. Intellectuals associated with these organizations revive antiquated and discredited economic theories extolling balanced budgets, sound money, and personal thrift, to support conservative policy positions and excel at bombarding media outlets, lobbyists, and congressional staffs with misinformation and flawed economic analysis.

Federal officials and elected representatives respond by bickering endlessly, even in the midst of a sharp economic downturn, about the need to cut spending and repay federal debt. The Federal Reserve and other central banks fixate on fighting inflation, though the inflation rate has declined steadily for over two decades. Officials of international lending agencies pressure governments around the world to place financial interests before other economic goals, even as their real economies have collapsed. The result has been a raw deal for the vast numbers of ordinary people, in the United States and elsewhere.

Each of the following chapters is an attempt to dispel the myths and illusions surrounding money, financial markets, federal finances, the financial policies of the Federal Reserve, and the policies of global financial institutions. At each turn, we will examine the myths promulgated in the media, the policies these myths engender, and the real impact these policies have on ordinary wage- and salary-earners.

Because the shifts in economic policy rest, to such a degree, on aligning the perceived interests of wage earners with financiers, chapter 2 will focus on the illusions surrounding the stock market and individual stock investing. Recent events shattered some, but not all, of those illusions. And recent corporate scandals have left Americans no less dependent on financial markets for funding retirement and higher education. I will argue that the stock market can never provide economic security for the majority. The problem is not simply that financial markets are volatile, or that they have been rigged by insiders. Rather, stocks and savings accounts provide middle-class households with no secure claim on the production of the real economy.

The politics of finance and money rest on a deliberate misrepresentation of government finances, fostering the belief that governments operate under restraints that are not, in fact, operative. Chapter 3 assesses the debates over federal borrowing, debt, and the prospects for Social Security.

The economic origins of our current impasse lie in the extraordinary power ceded to the Federal Reserve and other central banks in the 1980s and 1990s. Chapter 4 casts a critical eye on myths surrounding the conduct of monetary policy and the problem of inflation.

The economic consequences of the raw deal are today most evident in developing countries that, under the tutelage of the International Monetary Fund, geared their policies single-mindedly toward the protection of financial wealth. Chapter 5 looks at the role of the dollar in the world economy and the devastation that efforts to ensure the dollar wealth of international investors have wrought on the real economies of Asia and South America.

Chapter 6 offers suggestions for how to move beyond financial myths and construct policies that sustain and share the real wealth of the economy.

CHAPTER TWO

THE GREAT STOCK ILLUSION

Between 1980 and 2000, both the Dow Jones and Standard and Poor's indices of stock prices soared tenfold. The NAS-DAQ index, which follows the stock prices of newer businesses, had by the year 2000 skyrocketed to twenty-five times its 1980 level. As the bull stampeded through Wall Street, a fawning business press cheered from the sidelines, recounting tale after tale of intrepid dot-commers who had boldly forgone salary for stock in firms like E*Toys and Netscape and were now overnight millionaires.

Those too dense, too cautious or too unlucky to have ridden the Wall Street bull were urged to climb aboard, aided by an entire how-to industry selling stock tips, financial advice, and brokerage accounts for small investors anxious for a piece of the action. Web sites like E*Trade and Ameritrade offered discounted trading accounts and newspapers reported a surge in day-trading, where independent operators tried to beat the pros. Best-sellers with titles like *The Courage to Be Rich*, *The Millionaire Next Door*, and *Rich Dad, Poor Dad* promised to unlock the secrets of wealth. Cable TV provided round-the-clock financial gossip and breathless bull-market cheerleading on new channels like CNBC.

As the millennium approached, bullish expectations reached a feverish crescendo. Three separate books published in 1999 forecast further boundless appreciation in the stock market. *Dow 36,000: The New Strategy for Profiting from the Coming Rise in the Stock Market* sold out quickly. Next came *Dow 40,000: Strategies for Profiting from the Greatest Bull Market in History*. This was trumped by *Dow 100,000: Fact or Fiction*. Bullish Wall Street gurus like Goldman Sachs's Abby Cohen were quoted everywhere, insisting that prices could go nowhere but up.

Skeptics warned that it could not last. As early as 1996, Fed chair Alan Greenspan had fretted aloud that stock prices reflected more "irrational exuberance" than real economic value. Yale finance professor Robert Shiller, in a 2001 book itself titled *Irrational Exuberance*, warned that American equities were wildly overpriced. Compared with corporate earnings, stock prices in 2000 were higher than at any time in the past—higher even than before the 1929 market crash. Shiller, who for years had conducted surveys of professional investors, argued that market professionals were little better than anyone else at predicting the future course of stock prices. He attributed investor optimism to wishful thinking and self-fulfilling market sentiment, nourished by a culture that championed wealth and lionized the wealthy.[1]

Dean Baker and Marc Weisbrot of the Washington-based Center for Economic and Policy Research contended in

1999 that the United States' stock market looked like a classic speculative "bubble"—a kind of mania where enthusiastic investors pour funds into the market in hopes of instant wealth, blowing prices up, up, up until sentiment turns and the bubble bursts. As evidence they cited the rapidly diverging relationship between stock prices and corporate earnings and reckoned that, to justify the prices at which stocks sold in 2000, profits would have to grow at rates that were frankly impossible.[2]

The skeptics proved correct. Share prices plunged in the spring of 2000. The S&P index dropped 25 percent and the NASDAQ plummeted, losing over two-thirds of its value. Those holding shares in bull-market favorites like Cisco and Lucent suffered especially stinging losses. Cisco stock fell by 75 percent, Lucent by 95 percent. Today, chastened financial pundits acknowledge that stock prices were bid too high during the frenzied closing years of the twentieth century; that it will take years for corporate earnings to meet investors' bloated expectations; that stock prices will likely stagnate for a decade. This is bad news for middle-class households whose life savings languish in 401(k)s, individual retirement accounts (IRAs), and mutual funds. In 2001 and 2002 stock losses on the typical retirement account exceeded the combined value of new employer and employee contributions. Americans' savings disappeared into a black hole on Wall Street, leading many to wonder: where did all the money go? But most of the money never really existed in the first place. The phenomenal wealth promised by Wall Street was largely illusory.

THE ILLUSION OF MARKET DEMOCRACY

Before the 1980s, stock speculation had long been regarded as a rigged game for the idle rich. The public considered Wall Street the province of fat cats and greedy capitalists, and with its periodic waves of scandals and high-profile indictments, Wall Street routinely lived down to the reputation. But in the 1990s the finance industry's image got a boost. Advertisements for financial brokers and articles in the financial press portrayed high finance, critic Thomas Frank writes, as a "populist" arena where ordinary people, empowered by the Internet, could at last realize the American dream.[3] By 1998 more Americans owned stock than at any time in history, giving ordinary people a direct interest in the profitability of U.S. corporations. To promarket enthusiasts, this heralded an end to class conflict in the United States. With stock ownership widespread, some speculated that America had achieved a sort of decentralized socialism in which worker-shareholders owned the means of production. The *New York Times* columnist Thomas Friedman compared stock trading to democratic suffrage—the stock exchange a giant polling station where regular people "vote every hour, every day, through their mutual funds, their pension funds, their brokers, and, more and more, from their own basements via the internet."[4]

It is certainly true that, by the end of the twentieth century, stock ownership was more commonplace than at any time in the nation's past. According to historians, even in 1929, the last episode of stock mania, it is doubtful that more than one in five families had a stake in the market. By 1962, only 11 percent of households owned any stock at all. Today nearly half (49 percent) own some stock and those who do are entrusting more than half their savings to the stock market.

But ordinary middle-class workers are hardly in control of the nation's capital. Stock ownership—like ownership of all wealth—is intensely concentrated in very few hands. The Federal Reserve Board, which compiles data on wealth distribution every few years, estimates that 90 percent of all corporate stock (not to mention other assets like bonds and investment-trusts) is controlled by the richest one-tenth of American households. Even within this group, the really big bucks are held by a few families. Once we eliminate the merely affluent—professional families with six-figure retirement accounts—we find that half of all equities belong to just 1 percent of U.S. households. Just under 40 percent of all shares belong to the very richest one-half of 1 percent of households—about 250,000 families with an average net worth of at least $12 million.[5] This group, writes the former Republican campaign strategist Kevin Phillips, includes both the "deca-millionaires" and the "roughly 5,000 clans having assets of $100 million or more."[6] At the very pinnacle of the wealth distribution sit titans like Bill Gates, whose 800 million shares of Microsoft make him the wealthiest man in the world, with personal wealth estimated at around $50 billion.

In contrast, two in three U.S. households (those earning less than $50,000) owned little or no stock at all, according to the Federal Reserve. The typical portfolio for this group contained about $10,000 in stock in 1998, most of it held in retirement accounts. Collectively this group owned less than 4 percent of all corporate stock outstanding.

Because the wealthy own a disproportionate share of corporate stocks and because they have access to far better information on market trends, gains from the market flow disproportionately to the already rich. The economist Edward Wolff, who has made a career of studying wealth distribution, estimates that the richest 1 percent, though they own only half of all stocks, captured two-thirds of the gains generated by the bull market.[7] Thanks to stock gains and rising incomes, the wealthiest 1 percent doubled their share of the nation's wealth during the 1980s and 1990s—from 20 to 40 percent.[8]

Such extreme concentrations of wealth and stock ownership belie claims that the stock market is now the realm of the common man. If, as Thomas Friedman claims, Americans are casting "votes" in the pits of the New York Stock Exchange and over the wires of NASDAQ, then the voting is less akin to a Vermont-style town meeting than to the British parliament circa 1500. The Forbes 400—the stock market's House of Lords—get tens of millions of votes between them.

But what do they vote on? For middle-income households, this is not an idle question. While Americans of modest means garner an unusually small share of the gains during the market's ascent, they suffer disproportionately large losses as prices tumble. Ordinary families are caught up in the fortunes of Wall Street as never before and are increasingly vulnerable to the stock market's periodic bubbles and collapses. Yet ordinary American households remain marginal players on Wall Street, with virtually no control over how it operates and few votes of their own.

THE ILLUSION OF MARKET EFFICIENCY

In what sense is buying and selling stock, to use Friedman's analogy, akin to casting votes? Conventional Wall Street wisdom holds that when investors buy a company's stock, they are expressing confidence in the firm's future growth and profitability. A rising share price signals the "market's" favorable assessment of a company's products, policies, and plans for growth; a falling price conveys the market's displeasure with the firm's management. Financial commentators often interpret a general upsurge in stock prices as a vote of confidence in the U.S. economy—its dynamism, profitability, prospects for growth and expansion. From this perspective, it hardly matters how many Americans own shares; a buoyant market benefits all because all share in the prosperity that the market heralds.

Critics have far less faith in Wall Street's ability to distinguish good corporations from bad ones, never mind to foretell the course of the U.S. economy. A look at the market's record reveals some fabulous bloopers—from the crash of 1929 to the leveraged buyout craze of the 1980s to the dotcom and telecom bust of 2001. As Robert Shiller told the *New York Times*, "The idea that the market is going to reveal fundamental truths is nonsense. . . . The market has never predicted anything right."[9]

Whatever the market thinks it is voting about, there is no question that executives of U.S. corporations follow the votes closely, with serious consequences for their employees.

Until the 1980s, corporate managers had little direct contact with shareholders. Top executives did not generally own much stock in the firms they ran and, having little personal stake in the company, often disregarded the financial interests of the shareholder-owners. CEOs, for example, sometimes protected their own jobs and power by rejecting takeover bids, though a takeover would have lifted the share price. Executives retained profits for use by management rather than paying out dividends to stockholders. They delayed layoffs in the interest of employee morale and labor peace, but at the expense of profits.

Stockholders dissatisfied with a firm's management were free to sell their shares, but this too made little difference to management. The share price had little impact on the normal business operations of a company. Bankers might be reluctant to lend to a company whose share price was stagnant, but executives of large firms generally used retained profits to pay for expansion and so avoided borrowing anyway.

Beginning in the early 1980s, Wall Street insiders unleashed the so-called "shareholder revolution," a wave of aggressive and often hostile takeover bids justified on the grounds that they would compel executives to attend to stockholders. Shareholders, the story went, were the rightful owners of public corporations. Managers were mere employees—replaceable employees, at that—hired to maximize profits and increase the stock price. If managers pursued goals irrelevant to the shareholder's interests—preserving jobs, maintaining relationships with vendors, engaging in philanthropy—they should be driven out. Corporate "raiders" like Henry Kravis and Carl Icahn, together with financial whizzes like Michael Milken and Ivan Boesky, arranged dozens of "leveraged buyouts"—debt-financed merger bids—which, they claimed, would shake up recalcitrant executives.

Raiders borrowed huge sums on Wall Street, mostly in the form of unrated, high-yield "junk bonds"—heavily promoted by Michael Milken and his employer, Drexel Burnham. Flush with cash, raiders then bought controlling stakes in a targeted firm's shares and, once in control, ousted the old management, sold off divisions, and ruthlessly slashed costs to repay the debt. Wall Street economists argued that buyouts enhanced corporate efficiency. In a badly run company, the argument went, assets were not effectively deployed, so the market value of the whole firm was less than the sum of its parts. In buying the companies whole and selling off their parts, raiders not only enriched themselves, but enriched all society—ridding the economy of weak managers, featherbedding unions, and crony corporate cultures. As for the high-interest bonds used to finance these "raids," economists held that they too enhanced efficiency; to service the debt, the new, post-merger management team would be forced to operate a leaner, meaner, and more productive business. Or so the story went.

Others told a different story. Popular films like *Wall Street* and best-selling exposés like *Predators' Ball* and *Den of Thieves* contended that the money being made on hostile takeovers came not from improved efficiency, but from insider trading, corporate blackmail, and mistreatment of employees.[10] A company "in play"—the target of a takeover bid—was a sure bet for insiders who knew in advance that a raid would soon drive up the company's share price. Insider-trading charges rocked the financial industry in the late 1980s. Investigations by the Securities and Exchange Commission and by Rudolph Guiliani of the U.S. Attorney's Office uncovered intricate insider-trading schemes that funneled profits from illegal trades into secret offshore accounts. Milken and Boesky and other prominent financiers went to prison for insider trading and securities fraud. Drexel Burnham folded soon after.

In hindsight, economists found little support for the theory that raids made firms more "efficient." Companies that had been bought out, sold off, broken up, and restructured were no more profitable or efficient than other firms and in many cases were far less profitable. To repay the debts incurred by the raider, the new management team often sold the company's best-run (and most marketable) units, slashed research budgets, and discarded experienced employees. Share prices of restructured firms, though valuable in the midst of the buyout activity, did not remain high and often yielded longer-run returns inferior to the stocks of other companies.[11] Nevertheless, the shareholder revolution strongly impressed corporate managers. Managers learned that an underperforming share price invited unwelcome attention from takeover specialists and displeasure from their boards. Simply to forestall hostile bids and avoid being sacked, managers began concentrating on earnings and share prices.

The proliferation of executive stock options intensified this focus in the 1990s. Options, which enable the holder to buy shares tomorrow at today's price, are valuable only if the share price rises. By paying managers in options, corporate boards hoped to focus executives more directly on shareholder value. By the late 1990s, options accounted for an average 80 percent of the pay of top executives in U.S. public corporations. Options grants were frequently so large—involving in some cases hundreds of thousands or millions of shares—that a small uptick in price could make an executive exceedingly wealthy. A big price hike would catapult him into the Forbes 400. Given the staggering amounts of money involved, stock options directed executive attention on shareholder value like a laser beam. Executives grew obsessed with increasing reported earnings quarter after quarter to justify a higher and higher share price. Grateful boards showered those executives who "created shareholder wealth" with exorbitant compensation packages and, of course, with more stock options. Wealth and success in turn brought public acclaim and political influence to celebrity CEOs like General Electric's Jack Welch and Enron's Kenneth Lay.

Former energy-trading firm Enron is today in bankruptcy proceedings, its senior management under investigation, its accounting firm disbanded after being convicted of obstructing justice. Enron executives reportedly connived with big-five accountant Arthur Anderson to wildly overstate revenues and earnings and inflate the firm's share price. As the stock approached a peak of around $90 per share, executives exercised their options, enriching themselves at the expense of other shareholders who were left owning a bankrupt firm. *Wall Street Journal* reporter David Wessel writes that at Enron, "the incentives to do almost anything to increase the stock price were huge. And the incentives weren't to increase profits over a decade or two, but to increase profits . . . just long enough for executives to cash out." Nor were Enron's financial manipulations unique. As MIT economist Peter Temin told the *Journal*, "Everybody did this. The people who got in trouble are those who are most at the edge. Enron didn't get caught. Enron got so far out on the edge that it fell off."[12]

Recent history teaches that when firms are managed solely for shareholder votes, executives have every incentive to convert them into personal money machines. And until they fall off the edge, the brokers, bankers, traders, analysts, pundits, and economists on Wall Street stand on the sidelines cheering. Wall Street's voters turn out to have no special insight into the economy or the companies they vote on—no more insight, say, than union representatives, consumers, government officials, community residents, or line managers might exhibit. To create shareholder wealth, managers, as the business journalist William Greider puts it, "squeeze other contributors to a corporation's success—taking away real value from employees, suppliers, supporting communities and even customers."[13]

Yet shareholders get the votes and vote they do, on the world stock exchanges, in executive suites, and in private negotiations to buy, sell, merge, expand, and disband the corporations that employ millions of workers. Their votes, deal making, management fees, investment advice, and portfolio churning impact the lives of us all, and not necessarily for the better.

THE ILLUSION OF PUBLIC INFORMATION

In the bad old days of rugged, unrestrained, and unregulated capitalism, the days of trusts and combines, Wall Street was virtually synonymous with lawful thievery. From the late 1800s until the Great Crash of 1929, the market was dominated by cold-blooded insiders, and stock fraud was their weapon of choice. By spreading false information, watering down stock, issuing paper in nonexistent companies, or borrowing against stock they did not own, shrewd financial operators like Cornelius Vanderbilt, John D. Rockefeller, Jim Fisk, Daniel Drew, Jay Gould, and "Diamond" Jim Brady waged obscure financial battles for ownership of the nation's productive resources, manipulating stock prices and fleecing the unwary piker.[14]

In the wake of the financial and economic collapse of the 1930s, Congress established the Securities and Exchange Commission (SEC) to oversee stock trading and prosecute fraud. Companies that sold shares to the public were required to file audited financial reports with the SEC, documenting assets and sales. Insiders—those privy to important information about a company's finances—were prohibited from trading stock ahead of important public disclosures.

But requiring companies to file information did not mean that the information was easy to find or to understand. Corporate reports were not exactly laying around local libraries for casual perusal by a small investor. Even if they had been, few had the expertise to make sense of them. Before the explosion of mutual funds in the 1980s, a small investor wanting to play the stock market needed the guidance of professional insiders just to gather and interpret company data. Market pros frankly regarded the small investor as a chump. Many tracked the so-called Odd-Lot Index, a measure of small-scale (fewer than one hundred shares) trades. Reasoning that "the smallest traders don't know what they are doing," these pros took an uptick in demand from small investors as a sure sign that prices had peaked and it was time to sell.[15]

Small investors were further disadvantaged by the high fees professional brokers charged. Until fairly recently, most corporate equities were listed on organized exchanges —like the New York and American Stock Exchanges—and any purchase or sale of stock was conducted through a "specialist" on the trading floor. To buy or sell shares, one needed to engage the services of a broker with a seat on the exchange and access to the specialist. This was quite costly and gave established brokerages monopolistic control over transactions in listed corporations. Responding to lawsuits in the 1970s, the SEC outlawed fixed brokerage commissions in 1975 and competition from discount brokers soon broke the stranglehold of the major investment houses.

By the 1980s, Fidelity Corporation under Peter Lynch's leadership began heavily marketing mutual funds to middle-class households, allowing investors with moderate stakes to partake of the information, expertise, and access to exchanges of professionals, without investing time or worry in research and stock picking. Public access to stock ownership received a further boost in the 1990s, with the rapid expansion of the NASDAQ—an automated exchange and price-quotation system—and the arrival of rock-bottom discount brokers hawking their services over the Internet. By the late 1990s Web-based firms like E*Trade offered cheap instant-access on-line trading. The Internet also vastly increased access to corporate information; SEC filings for publicly traded companies are now available at the click of a mouse.

Since markets don't operate well unless relevant information is cheaply and widely available to buyers and sellers, a fundamental pillar of the great stock illusion was the notion, widely propagated by the media, that all relevant data needed for intelligent stock trading was available to anyone willing to look. Former Goldman Sachs vice president B. Mark Smith argued in his 2001 book *Toward Rational Exuberance* that the U.S. stock market by the late 1990s was more transparent, honest, and accessible to the small investor than ever before. Financial writers picked up on this theme, extolling the success of "investment clubs" like the Beardstown Ladies, who used public information and their own common sense to beat market pros and make a bundle.[16] Television commercials for Ameritrade featured a twenty-something tattooed techno-geek—the very antithesis of button-down Wall Street capitalists—instructing his stuffed-shirt boss in on-line trading. Slide the mouse, double click, instant wealth, anyone can do it.

But revelations unearthed by Enron's debacle have exploded this myth of perfect information. As Enron, WorldCom, Global Crossing, Tyco, and dozens of other firms self-destructed, the public discovered that profits and profitability are slippery concepts, that financial data is easily massaged by corporate insiders, that outside auditors routinely sell consulting services to the very firms they audit and, eager for the business, have been willing to overlook questionable transactions and sign off on financial statements that are deceitful if not fraudulent. They learned further that many Wall Street analysts—long regarded as the sole independent source of information on company performance—are corrupt, more concerned with drumming up business from the firms they analyze than protecting the interests of investors. It also turns out that financial pros—portfolio managers, mutual fund executives, brokers, planners, advisers—are no shrewder at detecting fraud than the average chump and that, when fraud is suspected, small investors are the last to find out.

As conditions deteriorated at Enron and at numerous other high-tech favorites like Lucent and Cisco, presumably

independent industry analysts at prominent financial firms
like Morgan Stanley, Salomon Smith Barney, and Merrill
Lynch were plugging their shares, issuing favorable reports
with strong-buy recommendations to unwary investors. At
the height of the bull market, when any rational analysis
suggested that prices had peaked and when serious allega-
tions of accounting irregularities were beginning to emerge,
fewer than 1 percent of analyst reports recommended that
investors sell a stock. At the time, Wall Street professionals
attributed this keyed-up bullishness to analysts' optimism
about emerging technologies. Investigations by New York
Attorney General Eliot Spitzer told a different story. As they
praised companies to investors, Merrill Lynch employees
were privately dismissing the same stocks as "crap" or
"junk" in internal e-mails and, along with company executives, quietly unloading the firm's own holdings on an un-
witting public.

Salomon Smith Barney analyst Jack Grubman actively
plugged Global Crossing and WorldCom shares until just a
month before the telecom behemoths filed for Chapter 11.
Grubman earned $20 million in 2001 for his part in steer-
ing telecom business to Salomon and resigned in August
2002 with $32 million in severance.[17] In 2003 he was under
investigation by the New York State Attorney General's
Office.[18] Merrill technology analyst Henry Blodget earned
his keep not by providing sound analysis to the firm's brokerage clients, but by courting corporate finance business
from the companies he analyzed. For "generating $115 mil-
lion in revenue from 52 deals . . . Blodget's compensation

quadrupled—from $3 million to $12 million—in 1999 and 2000," according to *Business Week*.[19] The *Wall Street Journal* reports that major investment firms routinely "wooed analysts with multimillion-dollar contracts based on their ability to generate investment banking fees" from the very firms that they were supposed to analyze.[20]

Enron alone paid $323 million in banking fees to Wall Street firms during the 1990s and was touted as a great buy all over the street.[21] Congressional hearings disclosed that Merrill, Citigroup, and other top banks helped set up, participated in, and profited from the partnership deals that were used to shovel cash out of the firm and led, ultimately, to its collapse. Enron's downfall was particularly devastating to its employees, who lost not only their jobs but also some $1.3 billion dollars in retirement savings. Managed by Enron executives, 60 percent of assets in the employee retirement plan were held in Enron shares.

During subsequent congressional hearings on Enron, a number of representatives attributed employees' losses to poor advice and financial understanding. Senator Joseph Lieberman of Connecticut wanted to encourage public financial literacy by offering tax incentives to companies that provide professional investment advice to employees. This presupposes, however, that professional advice is unbiased and not riddled with the conflicts of interest and insider corruption that recent investigations have exposed. Enron, as former Economic Policy Institute director Jeff Faux points out, "was touted by reputable financial analysts from the major investment houses, given accolades by professors at Harvard and other business schools. . . . Its books were certified by Arthur Anderson. And the biggest, most sophisticated investment banks in the world were lending the company billions of dollars."[22]

Sound information about stocks and the firms that issue them is and probably always will be the province of insiders—senior executives, the lawyers, consultants, and auditors in whom they confide, the investment bankers who advise them, the politicians who court them. During the bull market, major Wall Street banks gave favored telecom executives newly issued stocks in initial public offerings at the opening price, allowing the executives to profit richly when the price jumped.[23] In return, these insiders steered their own banking business to Wall Street. Small investors were locked out of such deals. Insiders like Martha Stewart sell ahead of bad news, legally and illegally; small investors get stuck holding the bag. Faux points out that, even in a booming stock market, small investors rarely obtain the returns that flow to the big players. "In a bull market, small investors get about one-third the average return on stocks and about half the average return on bonds. In a bear market they get hosed."[24]

Even when insiders are not deliberately deceiving them, small investors' stakes are liable to be eaten away by management fees. The U.S. Department of Labor, for example, found that mutual funds pile so many different fees on work-based savings accounts that "78 percent of plan sponsors did not know how much their costs were, largely because there are about 80 different ways in which vendors charge fees." In an investigative report for *Dollars and Sense*, James Ridgeway found that fees on employee savings accounts average 1.3 percent of an account's annual value, but can run as high as 3 percent.[25]

It's little wonder then that Edward Wolff, in the study of wealth distribution mentioned earlier, discovered that most American households actually lost wealth during the great bull market of the 1990s—virtually all the capital gains flowed to the top 10 percent of households. Most went to the top 1 percent.

THE ILLUSION OF WEALTH CREATION

And this, in fact, is how it must be. Not everyone can get rich, not even in a bull market—at least not unless the economy itself makes us rich.

As I have noted, what we collectively consume in any given year is limited by whatever goods and services the economy produces. If auto companies manufacture 5 million cars, consumers can buy 5 million and no more. If skilled surgeons can perform ten thousand knee replacements, then only ten thousand knees can be replaced. The "real economy"—the agglomeration of businesses and workers engaged in producing the things we actually use—sets an upper limit to the growth each year in the average standard of living.

Throughout the 1990s, the stock market promised wealth far in excess of what the economy was producing. In 1990 the combined value of all U.S. corporate equities amounted to a bit less than two-thirds of the nation's output, or gross domestic product (GDP). By 1999 stocks had more than quintupled in value; GDP increased about 60 percent. In 1999 alone, the total value of U.S. equities swelled by an astounding $4 trillion. During that same year, the real workaday economy increased its production of goods and services by only $500 billion—one-eighth of the increase in stock market "wealth."

What would have happened in 1999 if stock owners had all tried to realize such outsize wealth gains, to convert their $4 trillion in new stock market wealth into actual goods and services—homes, cars, clothing, and medical procedures? The answer is that most would have failed, because the economy did not in fact produce $4 trillion in new wealth. When investors scrambled to convert $4 trillion worth of paper into $500 billion worth of actual goods and services, most of the paper wealth would have dissolved. It would disappear because it never really existed in the first place, save as a kind of mass delusion.

Every time a share in, say, General Electric (GE) changes hand, the price at which the transaction took place is used to revalue all GE shares outstanding—just as the value of a home appreciates when the house down the block sells for more than a similar house sold last week. Homeowners understand that their real estate wouldn't be nearly so valuable if every house on the block were suddenly put up for sale. Similarly, if all 10 billion outstanding shares of GE—or even a small fraction of them—were placed on sale, they wouldn't fetch anywhere near the market price. The fact that some traders were bidding up the price of some stocks in the 1990s made everyone who owned stock feel rich. And neither the financial media nor American politicians, fascinated by the death-defying ascent of the market, noted the gaping disparity between the *claims* on wealth that stocks represented and the *actual* wealth that the economy produced. Indeed, CEOs who presided over soaring share prices were hailed for "creating wealth," when in fact they were creating simply the illusion of wealth.

Consider the case of GE. Under CEO Jack Welch, the company's shares rose nearly sixty-fold and Welch took full credit for "creating billions in shareholder wealth." When accounting scandals raised questions about GE's bookkeeping, half that wealth vanished. In fact, most of it had been chimerical in any case. If GE produced billions in wealth under Welch's reign, it resided in the high-quality refrigerators, air conditioners, appliances, and parts that GE's employees churned out year after year.

By the end of the decade, insiders were beginning to catch on to the widening disparity between the economy's output and the claims on that output represented by inflated stock prices. When they did, they rapidly attempted to liquidate their options and other stock holdings. Prices tumbled, wiping out trillions in illusory money.

Sellers who cashed out early did realize phenomenal returns. But given the limits on average consumption dictated by the real economy, their gains required that others necessarily received less-than-average income gains or even suffered losses. The arithmetic here is straightforward. When, through the exercise of inflated stock options and realization of inflated capital gains, some individuals capture real spendable income gains of 50 or 500 or 1,000 percent while the economy itself grows by only 3 or 4 or 5 percent, then the prosperity of the lucky few requires, in the short run, that others will gain nothing or even suffer losses. There are, after all, only so many goods and services to go around.

In any given year, millions of Americans receive windfalls and millions more find that their living standards lag behind the economy. It is no secret that market economies do not distribute income equally. Most of us accept inequality as the price of a dynamic economy, so long as inequities are not the product of deliberate manipulation by a particular group. Today, as greater numbers of U.S. households rely on the stock market to finance fundamentals like college and retirement, and as U.S. corporations make increasing use of stock to compensate executives or supplement employee 401(k) accounts, the stock market has come to play a critical role in how income gets distributed. And when economic rewards are allocated through the stock market, inequities become both systematic and deliberate.

When millions of shareholders rush to turn stock gains into real purchasing power, not everyone will succeed. Recent revelations clearly suggest that the winners are those with an inside track—those able to manipulate prices or information, those with inside knowledge, those able to control the timing of their employees' stock sales.

The case of Enron is the most notorious, but it is unfortunately not unique. When Enron filed for bankruptcy protection in November of 2001 its stock, which had traded as high as $90 per share a year before, plummeted to less than $1. *New York Times* reporter Jeffrey Seglin writes that the elevators in Enron's Houston headquarters sported TV sets tuned to CNBC, constantly tracking the firm's stock price and acclaiming the bull market generally. As Enron stock climbed in the late 1990s, these daily market updates made employees—whose retirement accounts were invested largely in company stock—feel quite wealthy. In fact, though, Enron workers were not free to sell most of this stock. The firm's contributions of company stock to employee retirement accounts did not vest until workers reached age fifty.[26] Because the stock had done so well on paper, many employees purchased Enron stock with their own 401(k) funds, over and above the firm's matching contribution. As the company disintegrated amid accusations of accounting fraud, even this stock could not be sold. For a full month before the bankruptcy filing, the company executives who managed the plan imposed a "blackout" on employee 401(k) accounts, so that workers were unable to unload even Enron stock they owned outright. With employee accounts frozen, Enron executives and board members dumped their own stock and options, netting an estimated $1.2 billion in cash—almost exactly the amount employees lost from their retirement accounts.[27]

As the stock market's performance in the late 1990s diverged from the real economy, small investors were assured repeatedly that stocks always paid off "in the long run"; that a "buy-and-hold" strategy couldn't lose. But insiders were rushing to the exits, trying to realize stock gains before the contradictions inherent in the market overwhelmed them.

Soon after Enron's collapse, telecommunications giant Global Crossing imploded amid accusations of accounting irregularities. Global Crossing's stock, which had traded at nearly $100 per share, became virtually worthless, but not before CEO Gary Winnick exercised his own options and walked away with $734 million. Qwest Communications director Phil Anschutz cashed in $1.6 billion in the two years before the firm stumbled under a crushing debt load; the stock subsequently lost 96 percent of its value. An investigation by the *Wall Street Journal* and Thomson Financial analysts estimates that top telecommunications executives captured a staggering $14.2 billion in stock gains between 1997 and 2001. "All told, it is one of the greatest transfers of wealth from investors—big and small—in American history," reporter Dennis Berman writes. "Telecom executives ... made hundreds of millions of dollars, while many investors took huge, unprecedented losses."[28] In 2003 the industry was reeling, with sixty firms bankrupt and five hundred thousand jobs lost.

Executives in the energy and telecom sectors were not the only ones to rake in impressive gains. Michael Eisner of Disney set an early record for CEO pay in 1998, netting $575 million, most in option sales. Disney stock later fell by two-thirds. Between 1999 and 2001 Dennis Kozlowski of Tyco International, who received an annual salary and other compensation valued at $30 million, reaped an additional $258 million selling Tyco stock. Kozlowski defended this windfall with the claim that his leadership had "created $37 billion in shareholder wealth." By the time Kozlowski quit Tyco under indictment for sales tax fraud in 2002, $80 billion of Tyco's shareholder wealth had evaporated.[29]

Fortune magazine analyzed over one thousand companies whose stock fell at least 75 percent between 2000 and 2002. It discovered that "executives and directors of the 1,035 companies took out . . . by our estimate, roughly $66 billion."[30]

Thanks mostly to the exercise of stock options, executive pay at the 365 largest U.S. corporations followed by *Business Week*'s Executive Compensation Scoreboard rose by an astonishing 340 percent during the 1990s—five times the rate of growth of economic output. In reporting their findings, *Business Week*'s writers concluded that "the market has made people wildly wealthy, none more so than chief executives at major U.S. companies."[31]

Media exposés uncovered dozens of lucrative deals that yielded extraordinary gains not only for executives but for board members, bankers, stock analysts, and politicians as well. Terry McAuliffe, chair of the Democratic National Committee, parlayed a $100,000 investment in Global Crossing into $18 million a few years later—a mind-boggling 17,900 percent rate of return.[32] Former Enron executive Thomas White sold some $10 million in Enron options in late 2001, while working as secretary of the army. Vice President Dick Cheney earned $36 million in 2000 from the sale of stock in Halliburton Corporation. During Cheney's stint as chief executive, Halliburton "altered its accounting policies so it could report as revenue more than $100 million in disputed costs on big construction projects," according to an investigation by the SEC.[33] The economist and *New York Times* columnist Paul Krugman unearthed information on a 1989 insider stock sale by George W. Bush. Bush, a member of the board and audit committee of Harken Energy, netted $848,000 just weeks before Harken admitted it had fraudulently booked $10 million in excess earnings. "An internal S.E.C. memorandum concluded that he had broken the law," Krugman writes, " but no charges were filed. This, everyone insists, had nothing to do with the fact that his father was president."[34]

The economic historian Robert Brenner estimates that executives and their boards fueled the bull market and kept share prices aloft by devoting billions in corporate profits and in borrowed funds to repurchasing their own outstanding stock. Between 1995 and 2000 over $1 trillion in corporate wealth was devoted to buying back the shares given out as executive options.[35]

THE ILLUSION OF RETIREMENT SECURITY

During the bull market, hundreds of U.S. corporations were stuffing employee savings accounts with corporate equity, creating a class of captive and friendly shareholders who were in many cases enjoined from selling the stock. Studies by the Employee Benefit Research Council found that, while federal law restricts holdings of company stock to 10 percent of assets in regulated, defined-benefit pension plans, 401(k)-type plans hold an average 19 percent of assets in company stock. This fraction rises to 32 percent when companies match employee contributions with stock and to 53 percent where companies have influence over plan investments.[36] Pfizer Corporation, by all accounts the worst offender, ties up 81 percent of employee 401(k)s in company stock, but Coca-Cola runs a close second with 76 percent of plan assets in stock. Before the firm went bankrupt, World-Com employees had 40 percent of their 401(k)s in the firm's shares.[37]

Contributions of stock are quite beneficial to corporations' bottom lines. Federal tax law allows firms to deduct the value of such contributions from their income when calculating profits reported to the IRS. But accounting conventions hold that firms need not deduct the value of contributed shares when reporting earnings to their shareholders. Financing employee retirement contributions with stock, rather than with cash, allows a firm to cut its tax bill while simultaneously inflating its bottom line. The boost to reported profits in turn props up share prices and the value of executive options.

Further, when the savings plans are structured properly, dividend payments—on which companies must ordinarily pay taxes—also become deductible for tax purposes, generating lucrative tax breaks for some nine hundred firms, including household names like McDonald's, Verizon, Anheuser-Busch, and Proctor and Gamble.[38] Such stock contributions cost firms virtually nothing in the short run and, since employees usually are not permitted to sell the stock for years, companies need not worry about diluting the value of equity held by important shareholders—or by their executive option-holders. Commenting on business lobbying efforts to gut proposed legislation that would restrict stock contributions to retirement plans, Marc Machiz, a former associate solicitor of the Labor Department in the retirement-plan security division, told the *Wall Street Journal*, "business loves having people in employer stock and lobbied very hard to kill this stuff."[39]

Before stocks fell in 2000–2001, most employees were untroubled by these trends. The market, after all, had been setting new records daily. Quarterly 401(k) statements recorded fantastic returns year after year. Financial advisers assured the public that stocks were and always would be good investments. But corporate insiders proved far less willing to bank on illusory stock wealth when securing their own retirements.

Pearl Meyer and Partners, an executive-compensation research firm, estimates that corporate executives eschew 401(k) plans for themselves and instead negotiate sizable cash pensions—the average senior executive is covered by a defined-benefit plan promising 60 percent of salary. Bernard Ebbers of WorldCom retired with an annual pension of $1.5 million before the firm collapsed in accounting scandals; the employee 401(k) plan was heavily loaded with company stock. CEO Richard McGinn quit Lucent at age fifty-two under pressure from the board with $12 million severance and a cash pension paying $870,000 annually. Lucent's employees, on the other hand, receive a 401(k) plan with 17 percent of its assets invested in Lucent stock. The stock plunged from $77 to $10 after McGinn's departure. By 2003 it was trading at under a dollar. Over seventy thousand Lucent workers had lost their jobs.

In addition to generous pension and severance arrangements, departing executives often negotiate lucrative in-kind payments. Jack Welch's retirement agreement specified that General Electric would provide "court-side seats at the U.S. Open, satellite TV at his four homes and the use of a GE-owned apartment on Central Park West, in addition to paying for laundry, wine, newspapers and other items associated with the apartment."[40] Louis Gerstner left IBM in 2002 with $14 million in pay and an estimated $400 million in stock options as well as a retirement package that promises "to cover car, office and club membership expenses for 10 years."[41] IBM's employees, in contrast, have been agitating since 1999 over the firm's decision to convert to a "cash-balance" 401(k)-type pension plan that, employee representatives estimate, will reduce pensions by one-third to one-half and save the firm $200 million annually.[42]

Surveying the impact of 401(k)s on employee retirement security, a *Business Week* report concludes that "CEO's deftly phased out rich defined-benefit plans and moved workers into you're-on-your-own 401(k)s, shredding a major safety net even as they locked in lifetime benefits for themselves."[43]

Corporate executives are also routinely provided with personal financial advisers at the firm's expense, who steer them away from the sorts of risks their employees typically bear. Meyer and Partners found, for example, that the more risky the industry and volatile a firm's stock, the more likely the firm's executives are to place their own savings in bonds and real estate. The typical executive owns real estate, for example, valued at between $5 and $10 million.[44]

In 1980 about half of U.S. workers participated in so-called defined-benefit pension plans, in which employers guaranteed retirees a fixed annual payment until death. Employee 401(k)s, along with cash-balance pensions, stock-ownership plans, Keogh plans, and so on, are known as defined-contribution plans, because they promise nothing more than the contribution that workers and (sometimes) their employers make into the plan. For holders of 401(k) plans, the benefit at retirement is undefined—it will depend upon the investment returns, the inflation rate, and how many years the money has to last.

Since 401(k)s were first introduced in the early 1980s they have grown explosively and have largely supplanted defined-benefit plans. Today, about half of U.S. workers have a retirement plan of some sort; the majority participate in a 401(k) or other defined-contribution plan. In 2002 three of every four dollars contributed to retirement accounts went into 401(k)s. It is thanks to 401(k)s and other retirement savings plans that middle-income Americans became stock owners in the 1980s and 1990s. It is also at least partly thanks to 401(k)s and the huge demand for stocks they generated that stock prices rose continuously in the 1990s.

And it will almost certainly be thanks to 401(k)s that the

problems inherent in using the stock market as a vehicle to distribute income will become glaringly apparent once the baby-boom generation begins to retire and attempts actually to liquidate its stock.

Financial planners routinely advise clients that a diversified portfolio of U.S. stocks has returned 7 percent—correcting for inflation and including dividend payouts—on average for the past one hundred years. This figure, derived from research done by the financial economist Jeremy Siegel, is the basis for very optimistic appraisals of American's retirement security.[45] Thanks to compounding—whereby the money one makes from an investment is itself reinvested to make even more money—paper wealth will multiply rapidly with a 7 percent annual return. Funds invested at 7 percent will just about double in ten years, then double again at twenty years, again at thirty years, and so on. According to this calculation, a twenty-two-year-old college graduate who put $5,000 in the stock market today would have about $90,000 at age sixty-five if returns averaged 7 percent. If she saved $5,000 each and every year and averaged a 7 percent return, she would be worth about $1.3 million at age sixty-five, plenty to finance a comfortable retirement.

There are a few hitches, however, to this scenario. First, there is the question of timing—stocks do fall in value, sometimes alarmingly, and there is no guarantee that our hypothetical college graduate will not retire just as the market tanks. Then there is the issue of risk—when calculating the future value of retirement savings, financial advisers will plug in a 7 percent return, blithely assuming that workers will toss their entire nest egg in the stock market. But stocks are volatile and risky, and even Siegel admits that a mixed portfolio of stocks, bonds, and liquid assets provides more dependable, but lower, returns.

But most worrisome is the presumption that the future will be like the past, despite ample evidence that times have changed. By Siegel's calculations, U.S. equities consistently outperformed not only all other financial investments like bonds, but also all other measures of economic output and income. Corporate stock prices have risen faster than corporate profits, faster than productivity, faster than corporate sales, and faster than the economy as a whole.

If stocks continue to rise at historical averages over the next ten years—something financial advisers routinely project and prospective retirees are counting on—the discrepancy between what the stock market promises and what the economy can deliver will widen dramatically. Something will have to give. Most likely what will give is the stock market itself—prices will plunge as retirees try to liquidate their holdings. Many will find themselves much less well off than they had imagined themselves to be.

The other possibility is that when the baby boomers retire, they will need to cash out their stock holdings just as younger workers, trying to finance their own future retirements, are sending fresh funds into the stock market. Stock prices, in this case, might hold steady. But if economic performance has not matched the stock market's performance, then retirees who succeed in realizing their paper gains will do so at the expense of younger workers who will be priced out of other markets, as retirees bid up the price of homes, medical care, and other necessities. When stock gains outstrip GDP gains for extended periods, we can expect to see a massive redistribution of income from nonshareholders to shareholders and from corporate outsiders to insiders.

Indeed, such trends were already evident in the stock boom of the 1990s. Income inequality fueled by stock options helped drive the price of a median home to over $600,000 in northern California and to over $500,000 in suburbs along the eastern seaboard.[46] Competition for spots in elite colleges has pushed annual tuition rates to over $30,000. High tuitions and declining need-based aid, according to *Business Week*, have opened a "yawning gulf in which post-secondary students from the richest quartile of families are nearly seven times as likely as those from the poorest families to earn a college-degree."[47] As employers pressure health insurers to reduce costs and insurers squeeze physicians to increase patient loads, the wealthy from Boston to Boca Raton are opting instead for "concierge care," paying up to $4,000 annually to gain access to physicians who limit their practice to a few hundred (well-heeled) patients.[48]

Institutional investors and financial economists have already begun to worry about the impacts of the baby-boom retirement on the stock market.[49] The trillions in retirement wealth may not be realizable. Of course, equity prices have outstripped profits and sales growth in the past without dire consequences. But in the past, few stockholders had cause to cash in their wealth. Since 1946, when the Federal Reserve began tracking such figures, annual net sales of equities have averaged a mere 0.02 percent of market value. In the past, stocks were rarely sold. When they were sold, economists found that households saved (or reinvested in other assets) virtually 100 percent of any gains they realized.[50]

This is because in the past, the typical shareholder was a wealthy family, a large corporation, or a well-endowed nonprofit institution. Such stock owners do not accumulate wealth with the intent of liquidating and consuming it in old age. The wealthy hold stocks, bonds, and other financial assets in trusts and endowments that are passed on to heirs. The goal is to preserve wealth, not to spend it, and so ensure a steady flow of interest and dividend income and a firm grip on status and power over generations.

Consider, for example, the Ford family. Heirs of founder Henry Ford control 40 percent of the voting shares of Ford stock. This arrangement gives them effective power over the board, power they used in 2001 to oust CEO Jacques Nasser and replace him with a family scion.[51] Bill Gates's 800 million shares of Microsoft stock give him dominance over the company. Equity holdings of this magnitude are rarely if ever liquidated, since selling amounts to forfeiting corporate control.

The various colleges of Harvard University together sit atop endowments valued at $19 billion; Yale has $10 billion and Princeton $8.4 billion.[52] The Ford ($14.7 billion), Rockefeller ($3.7 billion), and Carnegie ($1.9 billion) foundations, like most foundations and endowed institutions, rarely spend more than 5 percent of their endowments in any given year—the minimum required by law to maintain nonprofit status. Since returns on these endowments have, for twenty years, been far higher than 5 percent, this means that foundation assets, at least until the market sank, have grown larger. In this way, foundations have managed to preserve over decades much of the wealth of their robber baron founders. Following this tradition, Bill Gates recently transferred $21 billion to the newly established Gates foundation, headed by his father.[53]

American workers, however, are not accumulating 401(k)s for status or power or for their heirs. With the decline in traditional pension coverage, most will need to cash in every dollar of paper wealth to avoid penury in their old age. Yet stocks cannot rise faster than the economy grows, not if people are actually to live off the proceeds.

Or rather, stock prices cannot generate outsize returns unless corporate profits—on which stocks represent a legal claim—also surpass GDP gains. But for corporate earnings to consistently outpace economic growth, wages will have to stagnate or decline.

The pension economist Douglas Orr believes it is no accident that 401(k)s proliferated in a period of declining earnings and intense economic insecurity for most U.S. wage earners.[54] From 1980 until the mid-1990s the position of the typical American employee deteriorated noticeably. Wages fell, unemployment remained stubbornly high, benefits were slashed, and stress levels and work hours climbed as U.S. firms "downsized" and "restructured" to cut costs and satiate investor hunger for higher profits. Firms like General Electric cut tens of thousands of jobs and made remaining jobs far less secure in order to generate earnings growth that averaged 15 percent each year. CEO Jack Welch's ruthless union-busting and cost-cutting earned him the nickname "Neutron Jack" among rank-and-file employees. GE's attitude toward its employees was summed up by union negotiator Steve Tormey: "No matter how many records are broken in productivity or profits, it's always 'what have you done for me lately?' The workers are considered lemons and they are squeezed dry."[55] Welch was championed as a hero on Wall Street, his management techniques widely emulated by firms across the nation. During his tenure, GE's stock price soared as the firm slashed employment by nearly 50 percent.

GE was not alone. The Institute for Policy Studies, in a 2001 study, found that rising stock prices and soaring CEO pay packages are commonly associated with layoffs and that CEOs of firms that "announced layoffs of 1,000 or more workers in 2000 earned about 80 percent more, on average, than the executives of the 365 firms surveyed by *Business Week*."[56] Throughout the 1980s and 1990s, workers whose jobs were disappearing and wages collapsing consoled themselves by watching the paper value of their 401(k)s swell. With labor weak and labor incomes falling, wage and salary earners chose to cast their lots with capital. But in betting on the stock market, workers are in reality betting that wage incomes will stagnate and are trying to offset this by grabbing a slice from the profit pie.

This has already proved a losing strategy for most. Even at the peak of the 1990s bull market, the net wealth—assets minus debts—of the typical household fell from $55,000 to $50,000, as families borrowed heavily to protect their living standards in the face of stagnant wages.[57] The economist Edward Wolff found that, even at the inflated stock prices of 1998, the value of the typical 401(k) account did not compensate for losses that wage earners suffered in the general switch to defined-contribution plans. Wolff estimated that just over half of soon-to-be retirees would manage to achieve an adequate retirement income, compared with 70 percent in 1990. When the market dove, retirement savings plunged further. Stock market losses have caused the average 401(k) account to lose $13,000 since 2000, despite new contributions into the accounts.[58]

Until or unless the nation's capital stock is equitably distributed, there will be a clash of interests between owners of capital and their employees. If stocks and profits are routinely besting the economy, then either wage earners are lagging behind or somebody is cooking the books.

The entire 401(k) system is built on the promise of ever-rising stock prices, yet recent disclosures clearly show how unrealistic those promises will prove. At the outset of the bull market, corporate profits were growing at fantastic rates. But as job markets tightened in the late 1990s, wages picked up as well. By 1997, both profits and wages appeared to be rising at rates that surpassed the growth of GDP. Business commentators theorized that the federal government's economic data was flawed—that the old measuring sticks failed to capture the contribution of new technologies, that a "new economy" was now capable of enriching workers, bosses, and shareholders alike.

It now appears that much of this profit growth was illusory. Eager to please shareholders, corporations padded earnings by acquiring other companies (thus giving their bottom lines a short-term boost), by ill-conceived and often counterproductive reorganizations and layoffs, and by overstating earnings and understating expenses. Between 1999 and 2001, for example, Tyco reported a fivefold increase in earnings to triumphant applause from Wall Street. But these earnings were largely a mirage; by buying up several hundred smaller companies, Tyco was able to report rapid growth in earnings, though such growth could not be sustained except by continued acquisitions. Former *Harvard Business Review* editor Harris Collingwood contends that much of GE's growth in the late 1990s was not "generated by the brilliance of management or the diversity of their operations . . . but through the acquisition of . . . more than 100 companies in each of the last five years."[59]

A survey of middle-class investors conducted for *Business Week* found 60 percent of respondents agreeing that Enron was "an indication that well-known corporations have been using questionable accounting practices," and a further 28 percent felt that "there may be an epidemic of deceptive accounting practices involving many well-known corporations."[60] Their concerns are not misplaced. Since the failure of Enron, hundreds of U.S. corporations are being scrutinized for accounting irregularities. The economist Paul Krugman points out that during the late 1990s, "reported corporate profits soared, but the overall measure of profits calculated by the U.S. Commerce Department, which is unaffected by the maneuvers companies use to cook their books, hardly grew at all," indicating that book-cooking was widespread.[61]

Energy trading firms like Dynergy and Enron reportedly bought and sold electricity contracts from and to each other simply to create the illusion of trading activity and revenues. Executives of drug store chain Rite-Aid Corporation were recently indicted for overstating earnings by $1.6 billion. Xerox, which paid $10 million in fines for deceptive accounting, was one of 150 U.S. firms forced to restate earnings for 2001—triple the level of restatements in prior years. Telecommunications behemoth WorldCom admitted to booking routine expenses as capital expenditures and to smoothing earnings with cash reserves, exaggerating its profits by a staggering $7.2 billion. WorldCom's apparently phenomenal earnings led competing firms like AT&T to pressure its own managers for comparable results.

None of this bodes well for retirement savings. Yet surveys show that Americans like 401(k)s. In part, this is because savings accounts are portable, an important consideration in a world where workers can expect to change jobs several times over their working lives. But partly it is because savings plans provide the illusion of self-sufficiency and independence. When retirees spend down their savings, it feels as if they are "paying their own way." They do not feel like dependents, consuming the fruits of other people's labor. Yet they are. It is the nature of retirement that the aged opt out of production and rely on the young to keep the economy rolling. Pensions are always a claim on the real economy—they represent a transfer of goods and services from working adults to nonworking retirees, who no longer contribute to economic output. The shift from defined-benefit pensions to 401(k)s and other savings plans in no way changes the fact that pensions transfer resources, but it does change the rules that will govern how those transfers take place—who will pay and who will benefit.

Private defined-benefit pensions impose a direct claim on corporate profits. In promising a fixed payment over a number of years, corporations commit to transfer a portion of future earnings to retirees. Under these plans, employers promise an annual lifetime benefit at retirement, the amount determined by an employee's prior earnings and years of service in the company. How the benefit will be paid, where the funds will come from, whether there are enough funds to last through a worker's life—this is the company's concern. Longevity risk—the risk that a worker would outlive the money put aside for her retirement—falls on the employer. Retirees benefit from a secure payment, but at a cost to shareholders. Similarly, public pension programs, whether through Social Security or through state and federal civil service plans, entail a promise to retirees at the expense of the taxpaying public.

Today, the vast majority of workers, if they have pension coverage at all, participate in defined-contribution plans, in which they and their employer contribute a fixed monthly sum and invest the proceeds with a money-management firm. At retirement, the employee owns whatever funds have accrued in the account and must make the money last until he or she dies. Defined-contribution plans are a direct claim on nothing. Workers are given a shot at capturing some of the cash floating around Wall Street, but no guarantee that they will succeed.

Employee 401(k)s will add a huge element of chance to the American retirement experience. Some will sell high, some will not. Some will realize gains. Some will not. If the economy has not grown enough to supply the resources that retirees demand when they liquidate their savings, then income will necessarily be redistributed—either stock prices will decline as people try to convert wealth into income, or those who successfully convert paper gains to income will bid up the prices of housing, health care, prestige colleges, and other relatively scarce goods.

Pearl Meyer and Partners estimate that outstanding, unexercised executive stock options and employee stock incentives in 2003 amounted to some $2 trillion. Any effort to cash in this amount, in addition to the stock held in retirement accounts, would have a dramatic impact on stock prices. American workers and retirees, in assessing their chances for coming out ahead in the competition to liquidate stock, might ponder this question: If, as employees in private negotiations with their corporate employers, they have been unable to protect their incomes or jobs or health or retirement benefits, how likely is it that they will instead be able to wrest gains from Wall Street, where corporate insiders are firmly in control of information and access to deals?

CHAPTER THREE
DEBT DELUSIONS

In our winner-take-all economy, the prices of goods that are most critical to our sense of well-being—unhurried doctors, high-quality schools, homes within a reasonable commuting distance to the workplace—escalate uncontrollably when the economic elite, armed with outsize incomes, bid for them. The limits imposed by the production of the real economy dictate that success for the few brings distress for the many. The individualized money economy offers no rational coping strategies, beyond competing for a super-size income of one's own. And the markets most impacted by this competition are those to which we entrust our health and the health and welfare of our children and parents.

There is another alternative. It consists not in giving everyone his own pot of gold to throw into the market and compete with the insiders, nor in regulating the insiders and preventing fraud. Both of these solutions—spreading the wealth through expanded IRAs and tax-sheltered savings accounts and tightening up accounting and securities rules—which have considerable bipartisan support in Congress, are useful and needed, but they will not significantly improve the lots of ordinary households.

The government should indeed regulate these markets, insist on more forthright disclosure, prosecute fraud, and help individuals negotiate the market through financial advice and sheltered savings plans. People need money and a safe way to save it. But when all is said and done, the typical wage or salary earner is less well served by money than by institutions that minimize the importance of money in dictating fundamental living standards.

Financial wealth loses its significance when valuable and expensive services like pensions, health care, and education are provided through collective institutions. Federal pension systems, state colleges, and government health insurance greatly reduce the exposure of ordinary people to financial risks. Costs that are overly burdensome and unpredictable for an individual or family, like those associated with raising a child, treating a chronic illness, or outliving one's savings, are instead dispersed across the population. Access is based upon political criteria—whether one works, pays taxes, is a citizen—rather than on how much wealth one has accumulated.

Even the most fervent free-market economists acknowledge that markets fail to provide some services equitably or well. Economists say that a market is efficient when producers provide a good at a price that is in line with cost and when they respond to heightened demand with greater production. Efficiency is unlikely unless a number of elements are in place: Consumers must have pertinent information. They must be in a position to assess their economic interests and make rational choices. They must be able to opt out of the market if their interests are not being served. They must have sufficient income and be willing to pay for a service, and not simply ride for free on someone else's tab. Producers must face competition for their service. They must be willing to step up production in response to higher prices. In addition, civic stability demands that markets not violate basic societal norms of fairness and human dignity. Few markets meet all these criteria and some meet virtually none.

Health care, for example, fails on numerous counts. Patients lack essential information about appropriate medical care. They are rarely in a position to make informed and reasoned choices and often unable to walk away. Production is not flexible, because a limited number of medical school and residency slots restricts the pool of licensed providers. Perhaps most important, society has strong social and moral interests in ensuring that all receive adequate care, interests that are largely unmet in a society without universal health care coverage.

Other markets fail for similar reasons—childcare, eldercare, access to clean water. Real estate markets are plagued by problems of inflexible supply, especially in cities and recreational regions where proximity to transport or beaches, for example, is necessarily limited. Pharmaceutical markets, due to exclusive patent protection, lack sufficient competition, an important cause of escalating drug prices. Education and old-age pension markets are hampered by low consumer incomes as well as by powerful ethical concerns over quality and equity.

This is why many essential services are so rarely bought and sold on unregulated, profit-driven markets. Even in the United States—the least socialistic of all major economies—education at all levels is operated either by governments or by nonprofit institutions. Concerns over equity even drive local governments to supplement a thriving private market in books with public libraries. Health care in the United States was long provided by independent physicians, bound by a professional code of ethics, and by public or not-for-profit hospitals and insurers. For-profit chains began buying into the health care system in the 1990s, but suspicions about their motives fueled intense public dissatisfaction with the U.S. health system and recent studies confirm that they offer inferior care.[1]

When a good or service is fundamental to human dignity, citizens in democratic countries have generally voted to remove it from the money economy altogether. This is not communism, but a simple recognition that markets fail and citizens must band together to correct these failures. European governments, bowing to popular pressure, have since the 1950s provided comprehensive health care, dental care, childcare, and eldercare to their citizens. Education, though restricted by testing and tracking in the secondary schools, is cheap or free through the college level. Old-age pensions are munificent, replacing from 50 percent (in France) to 75 percent (in Germany) of preretirement earnings. The U.S. Social Security system, in contrast, replaces only one-third of prior earnings on average. Unemployment insurance is also generous, designed to spread the distress of economic downturns broadly among the population. Swedes, Danes, and Norwegians, for example, receive as much as 90 percent of prior earnings for up to a year after losing a job. In the United States, by contrast, unemployment insurance replaces less than one-third of prior earnings and eligibility is so restricted that nearly two-thirds of unemployed workers receive no benefits at all. Social insurance programs relieve middle-class Europeans of the need to save up and pray for high financial returns, since so much of what is essential to security has been removed from the money economy. The high and highly progressive taxes that support these programs further ensure that the fruits of economic growth will be widely shared, that income gains from the real economy are a sure thing rather than a crapshoot.[2]

Americans are often said to view things differently, to prefer to deal with economic stresses individually rather than collectively. But polls do not support this argument. When queried about U.S. health, education, or retirement policies, overwhelming majorities express support for more, not less, government. Pollsters have found that 77 percent of Americans believe the government should spend more on health care and 67 percent think it should guarantee health coverage for all. Eighty-nine percent want Medicare to pay for prescription drugs and two in three Americans want more tax dollars spent on mental health. Even after September 11, 2001, when terrorism and security concerns dominated, people consistently ranked Social Security, health, and education among their top five political priorities. When asked about educational priorities, large majorities favor federal spending to reduce class sizes, train teachers, and upgrade facilities.[3]

Voter sentiment on these issues, while constantly pandered to, is routinely neglected. Even the most conservative, antigovernment politicians campaign with promises to bolster Social Security, expand Medicare, improve schools, and reform health care. George W. Bush, perhaps the most probusiness president the country has had since the 1920s, could never have been elected had he not run as a "compassionate conservative," an admirer of Franklin Roosevelt and zealous defender of New Deal programs. Once in office, though, Bush, like Clinton before him and like hundreds of Democrats and Republicans in Congress since the 1980s, backpedaled almost immediately.

The difficulty, Americans are told, is that our nation—the richest in the world, indeed the richest country that the world has ever seen—is broke, burdened by past mismanagement with a crippling debt. And until the debt is paid, or reduced, or somehow addressed, which never seems to happen, voters' dreams must be deferred.

THE MYTH OF THE BURDENSOME DEBT

In 1989 the real estate developer Seymour Durst spent $150,000 to install the National Debt Clock—a ticking time bomb prominently displayed in New York's Times Square that tracked the federal debt minute by minute.[4] Billionaire entrepreneur Ross Perot ran for president as an independent candidate in 1992 promising, among other things, to get the nation's balance sheet back in the black. With backing from several wealthy businessmen, the Concord Coalition was founded in 1992 to promote policies and politicians committed to debt reduction and to "advocate fiscal responsibility." Dozens of books and articles appeared decrying the debt's "burden on future generations." In his top-selling 1988 book, *The Day of Reckoning*, the economist Benjamin Friedman opened each chapter with ancient moral injunctions against borrowing and lending.

If stocks awaken fantasies of instant wealth, debts unleash nightmares of financial ruin. The Times Square debt clock read $5.7 trillion when it was briefly dismantled in 2000 and $5.9 trillion when it was reinstalled in 2002. By 2003, it had climbed to $6.8 trillion. Lest passersby fail to grasp the magnitude of that number, Durst's clock does the arithmetic for them—$6.8 trillion divided among the U.S. population works out to $23,336 for every man, women, and child. The clock clearly implies that one day these hard-pressed Americans will be asked to pony up, and if they do not pay, the debt will swell to torment their children and grandchildren.

But this will never happen. Debts of the federal government differ entirely from personal debts; they do not need to be repaid, are not claims on the incomes of ordinary families, and will not plague future generations. While it is true, in a vague and general sense, that "we" owe this money, it is also true, as any introductory economics textbook will explain, that we owe it mostly to ourselves. Yet antigovernment groups prey upon the public's understandable anxieties concerning debt to garner support for policies anti-thetical to the public's interest.

When the federal government runs a deficit in its annual budget—spending more than it collects in revenue—it closes the gap by selling promissory notes (called T-bonds and T-bills) to the financial markets. The national debt is the accumulated value of these notes. Wealthy institutions and individuals—mostly banks, insurance companies, pension funds, mutual funds—with extra cash on their hands buy the notes in return for the promise of regular interest income and repayment when the notes come due or mature.

Of the $6.8 trillion in notes outstanding in 2003, about $600 billion were held in the Federal Reserve Bank as backing for the U.S. money supply. That $600 billion can be excluded from our reckoning of the debt. The Fed does not expect to be repaid and it returns most of the interest it earns to the U.S. Treasury at the end of each year.[5] Another $2.7 trillion is held by agencies of the various branches of government (most by the Social Security Administration, as discussed below). That leaves about $3.5 trillion owed to private institutions and individuals. These notes do indeed come due and bondholders expect timely repayment. But all involved in these markets understand that as the bonds and bills mature, the Treasury simply "rolls them over"—selling freshly issued notes to new buyers and using the cash to repay the maturing debt. Buyers are never in short supply. U.S. Treasury securities are one of the world's safest investments, better than cash because they pay interest, but safe as cash since, like dollars, they are obligations of the U.S. government.

Default is unthinkable. If the Treasury were to default—failing to make timely repayments or interest payments on its notes—it may just as well declare the dollar worthless and the government in crisis. Money, after all, is also debt of the U.S. government—or at least a liability on its balance sheet; defaulting on federal bonds would be equivalent to withdrawing the full faith and backing of the government from the U.S. money supply.[6] Because the dollar is used worldwide, a U.S. default would destabilize not only the U.S. financial system, but financial markets throughout the world. In the spring of 2002 Democratic congressional leaders balked at raising the statutory debt ceiling—effectively denying the Treasury's legal authority to borrow and roll over its debts—insisting that the Bush administration "submit a revised budget" or at least admit its current budget was "off-course."[7] Since failing to roll over its maturing bonds would technically have placed the U.S. Treasury in default, all concerned recognized the Democrats' threat as political grandstanding. Had Congress actually forced a default, this would have been the economic equivalent of a coup d'état.

Repaying federal debt is equally unpalatable, though government officials love to think about it aloud. During his last years in office, Clinton vowed to repay the debt and "make America debt-free for the first time since the Civil War." Most voters would dearly love to clear debt from their own balance sheets, so debt repayment carries intuitive appeal. But if the United States has been in debt for 140 years with no ill effects, skeptics might wonder why repayment is suddenly so urgent. Bondholders certainly are not clamoring for repayment. In fact, without U.S. Treasury bonds to invest in, banks, insurance firms, pension fund trustees, and other financial managers would lose their safest and most negotiable (easily bought and sold) financial asset. The Fed would lose the ability to introduce money cheaply into the banking system. Retirees would lose their best alternative to putting savings in the unpredictable stock market.

Repaying debt would probably make the stock market (and thus retirement accounts) even more volatile. The Treasury would need to collect excess taxes—thereby reducing households' disposable income—and transfer the excess revenues to the wealthiest 1 percent of the population, who hold half of all bonds. Chapter 2 provided a good preview of what the wealthy would do with this windfall. There is more. If pursued zealously, debt repayment might trigger an economic depression. With less income at their disposal, consumers and businesses would be forced to curb spending on U.S. output, the motor that keeps the economy chugging.

Before the 1940s, financial bubbles, crashes, scandals, and scams often devastated economies. When asset prices plunged, people lost savings, defaulted on debts, and curtailed spending plans. Financial firms and their wealthy clients refused to write new loans or buy new stock for fear of incurring more losses. Manufacturing businesses could not borrow to maintain production. Consumers could not borrow to keep up their own spending. Cash dried up. Businesses failed. Workers were thrown out on the street. After the stock market crash of 1929, eight hundred banks failed, leaving some 9 million depositors empty-handed. Thousands of businesses folded and millions of jobs disappeared. U.S. Steel alone laid off 225,000 workers between 1930 and 1933. Historians estimate that between one-quarter and one-third of workers were unable to find jobs. Wages plummeted to as little as five cents an hour. Half of all mortgages were foreclosed. The U.S. economy collapsed, with production declining by 50 percent.

In a monetary economy, where money is required to facilitate every transaction from buying bread to paying employees, financial crises can be calamitous. The country's buildings and factories still stand, the land is still fertile, and the people still seek work, but without money to set everything in motion the economy grinds to a halt. A national government, though, has the ability to prevent financial crises from damaging the real productive economy.

In the 1930s the British economist J. M. Keynes urged governments to use their unique ability to print or borrow money to combat the Depression. By borrowing funds that investors were reluctant to lend to private businesses, governments could jump-start factories and employ idled workers. "Fiscal stabilization policy," as Keynes's followers later termed this, required elected officials to jettison years of conservative doctrine on the virtue of balanced budgets. Putting people to work required governments to run deficits and pile up debts. The debt, Keynesian economists argued, did not matter. It was simply an accounting entry—a loan to the public from the public—whose economic function was to transfer idle resources from the wealthy to the broad citizenry.

THE DEATH OF THE KEYNESIAN CONSENSUS

The 1930s launched the "Keynesian Revolution." Roosevelt's New Deal included large-scale public works and income-support programs financed through federal borrowing, the first instance of peacetime deficit spending in U.S. history. But Roosevelt's efforts to develop federal jobs programs like the Work Projects Administration and Civilian Conservation Corps were fraught with controversy and fiercely contested. Actual New Deal spending was relatively timid—the federal deficit never reached $4 billion even at the peak of the New Deal—and unemployment rates remained intractably high throughout the decade, rarely falling below 20 percent.

Hostility to Keynesian ideas in the 1930s, though, could not survive the evidence of World War II. Thanks to a tenfold increase in federal spending, the U.S. economy went from deep depression to rapid boom virtually overnight. The government's deficit swelled to $47 billion in 1944 and its debt multiplied sixfold. Immediately after the war, the U.S. Congress passed the Employment Act of 1946, committing the federal government to "provide the maximum employment, production, and purchasing power."

Support forged in wartime for federal involvement in

economic matters proved hard to sustain once the war ended. Although tepid and watered-down compared with postwar European programs or to Keynes's own proposals, New Deal–type programs were sufficiently socialistic to galvanize unending hostility in the deeply conservative probusiness arena of U.S. politics. Continued government spending after the war faced determined opposition from businesses, which decried swollen government budgets as "creeping socialism" and complained that government programs amounted to "unfair competition" with the private sector. In 1954 the radical economist Harry Braverman pronounced Keynesianism in the United States "deader than the dodo."

Conservatives supported the federal highway program, cold war military buildup, the Korean and Vietnam Wars, but they did not support the deficit financing of these ventures, nor did they back the use of federal deficits as tools of economic management. By the early 1960s, even moderate gestures toward fiscal stabilization had become a hard sell in Congress. Keynesian economists worried openly about "implementation lags"—the yawning gap between the onset of a recession and the time it might take Congress to do something for the unemployed.

Throughout the 1960s and 1970s coalitions of liberals and moderates tried to stem the backlash, quietly constructing a political and intellectual infrastructure that would weave some basic fiscal stabilization into the fabric of federal law. Under the Johnson and Nixon administrations, federal entitlement programs—Social Security, Medicaid, Medicare, food stamps, child nutrition programs, and a plethora of welfare programs—were enacted or vastly expanded. Economists called these automatic stabilizers, because, as enacted, eligible applicants could not be denied benefits for lack of budgeted funds. Mandated spending levels would rise and fall predictably with the unemployment rate.

Entitlements legally committed the government to increase spending during economic downturns, regardless of the impact on the deficit and despite congressional opposition to Keynesian fiscal policies. These programs were neither massive nor generous—especially as compared with their European counterparts—but taken together they provided a bedrock level of federal spending in lean years as well as a minimal guaranteed income to prevent wages (and consumer spending) from plummeting in a recession.

With the sole exceptions of Reagan's and George W. Bush's tax cuts and military buildups, automatic increases in entitlement spending and sharp decreases in progressive tax revenues during recessions had been the major source of fiscal stimulus in the United States since 1973. They continue to be a major source of fiscal policy, though cuts in social programs and a flatter income tax system are making automatic stabilizers far less effective. During the recession of 1991, for example, virtually all of the $47 billion increase in the federal deficit came about because of declining tax receipts combined with increased welfare, unemployment, and Social Security spending. During the recession of 2001–2002, sharp declines in tax receipts caused the federal deficit to increase by some $160 billion. Bush's additional tax cuts and spending programs swelled the deficit to nearly $500 billion by 2003.

Keynesian-trained economists insisted that when recessions suddenly swelled welfare and Social Security rolls and cut tax receipts, the resulting deficits should not really count as deficits at all. Beginning with Herbert Stein, chairman of the Council of Economic Advisers under Nixon, government economists carefully distinguished between "structural" or "high-employment" deficits—where the government's budget was out of balance even in a booming economy—and "cyclical" deficits—where the deficit swelled unavoidably due to rising entitlements and falling tax collections. Through deficits, the government could maintain a basic level of income and economic activity, averting the downward spiral that might result if unemployed workers were forced to curtail spending, triggering more layoffs. "Full-employment budgeting"—the position that balancing the federal budget should take a backseat to expanded financing of entitlements during a recession—sustained Keynesian fiscal policy during the Reagan-Bush years and despite their opposition.

Before the 1930s, the U.S. government had faithfully matched spending to tax receipts each year unless the nation was at war. After the New Deal, fiscal deficits became a fixture of federal budgeting. The Treasury ran deficits from 1934 until the end of World War II, accumulating a public debt by 1946 equal to 120 percent of U.S. GDP. In fact, efforts to rein in spending after the war probably set off the first postwar recession in 1948. Political conflict over federal spending intensified during the 1950s and, under pressure from congressional conservatives, the government ran small surpluses in 1951, 1956 and 1957, and 1960. These bouts of fiscal virtue generally preceded an economic slump, confirming Keynesian warnings that deficits promoted growth while surpluses triggered depressions.

The Kennedy and Johnson administrations borrowed to pay for the Vietnam War and the expansion of social programs known collectively as the Great Society during the 1960s, a period of rapid growth and exceptionally low unemployment. Conservative backlash restored budget balance in 1969 and may also have provoked the end of the decade-long 1960s boom. No wonder that Richard Nixon, pondering his chances for reelection in 1972, declared "we are all Keynesians now" and oversaw further expansion of federal spending and deficit financing.

In fact, from 1969 until 1998 the U.S. government spent more than it took in each year. When economic booms generated rising tax receipts, fiscal conservatives attempted to hold on to the revenues and repay debt. But these sporadic episodes of fiscal discipline never lasted—most heralded the onset of recession and the sudden reversal in the government's fiscal position.

THE CROWDING-OUT MYTH

Economists cite two potential ills that might result from deficits and the subsequent rise in public debt. First, private firms desiring to borrow from the financial markets could find themselves "crowded out" by competition from the U.S. Treasury. Competition for scarce funds might drive up interest rates and depress business spending on new facilities and equipment. Further, if the government's spending draws too heavily on a finite pool of workers, materials, and other resources, prices and wages might rise, causing inflation.

During the 1990s, as the political tenor of both the country and the economics profession grew more conservative, authors of standard college economics texts elevated these precautions to absolute admonitions against deficit spending. A 1997 text by the Harvard economist and Bush economic adviser Gregory Mankiw, heavily promoted as the authoritative voice on contemporary economic thinking, maintained with no caveats that government borrowing uses up a limited supply of national savings, driving interest rates up until "it crowds out households and firms who would otherwise borrow to finance investment."[8]

But statistical studies find a weak or no correlation between deficit spending and interest rates.[9] The late economist Robert Eisner pointed out that, if crowding out were really a problem, it would occur with or without deficits. After all, if government programs are financed through higher taxes instead of borrowing, "then the IRS would be taking those funds instead; they would still not be available for business loans." Eisner contended and research confirmed that deficits are more likely to "crowd in" new investment by creating jobs, stimulating spending, and providing the roads, research, education, and infrastructure to support business expansion. Economic expansion in turn elevates tax collections and shrinks subsequent deficits. Studies by the Congressional Budget Office found that "the short-term effect of a one percentage point drop in the unemployment rate is a drop in the deficit of about $40 billion."[10]

Governments borrow in good economic times, bad times, and in mediocre times. They borrow when interest rates are high and when they are low, in periods of rising prices, stable prices, and falling prices. Scholars have attempted to confirm the crowding-out effect, without success. Interest rates seem to depend less on the government's fiscal position than on actions of central banks like the Federal Reserve. The economist James Galbraith points out that when Congress and the Clinton administration cut the U.S. deficit dramatically in the 1990s, fully expecting interest rates to plunge, the Federal Reserve instead "doubled the short term interest rate . . . and the notion of any link between deficit cutting and interest rate reduction was decisively nullified."[11]

Concerns that deficit spending by itself causes inflation also find little support in the data. In fact, the argument that government borrowing uses up scarce resources, drives up prices, and crowds out private activity is ultimately a political, not an economic, position. Public programs will crowd out private aspirations only when the private economy is fully utilizing the economy's resources. If workers are unemployed and factories idle, public programs can only benefit the economy. But even in a period of economic growth, what is so ruinous about crowding out? If the private sector fails to provide services that voters want and need, should we object when the government steps in to fulfill these needs? The dread of crowding out masks a deeper conviction among conservatives that services provided by the government are inferior to those provided by private businesses, a certainty that resources taken for public use are resources wasted. When deficit hawks oppose publicly funded long-term care for the elderly or childcare for working mothers on the grounds that they would generate deficits and crowd out private initiatives, they are arguing, in effect, that the health needs of elders and care needs of children would be better served by private markets than by the public sector. Opposition to federal deficit spending is used to camouflage opposition to federal spending on programs that benefit working Americans.

Rarely, however, will opponents state this unequivocally. Whether in economic textbooks, think-tank papers, or legislative debate, antagonism to public spending is carefully couched in the technical language of finance. Political opposition to a more vibrant and responsive public sector is disguised as hardheaded economic realism.

A second and more serious objection to deficit spending is that continual federal borrowing breeds a burgeoning public debt and with it, rising interest obligations to lenders. Eventually, some worry, the interest commitments grow onerous, absorbing an ever rising share of the federal budget. But this again raises issues more political than economic in nature. There is no reason that rising interest obligations should crowd out other federal programs except for the fact that antigovernment conservatives attempt to set artificial caps on the level of federal spending. Interest payments can, in any event, best be held down through monetary policy—printing sufficient money to keep banks flush with cash and interest rates low.

Interest payments do, however, raise distributive concerns. Bonds are held mostly by financial institutions and wealthy individuals. Some analysts worry that federal interest obligations transfer too much income from middle-class taxpayers to affluent bondholders. A detailed study by Colgate University economist Thomas Michl found, however, that while the very wealthy hold a disproportionate share of federal debts, government security holdings are less concentrated than other financial assets (like stocks). Further, interest is taxable income and the wealthy face relatively high federal tax rates. Michl estimated that, when these factors are accounted for, only 13 percent of federal interest payments involve an upward redistribution of income.[12]

Nevertheless, spiraling debt and burgeoning interest obligations probably are not the best way to manage a federal budget. National deficits and public debts can play a vital role in preventing unemployment and promoting economic growth. When the private economy booms, public programs should probably be financed by taxes. Unfortunately, though, intelligent debate about public spending or taxes has, in the U.S political arena, been drowned out by shrill rhetoric about deficits.

DEFICIT POLITICS

Ronald Reagan campaigned for the presidency in 1980 on a platform dubbed "supply-side economics." Coined by the *Wall Street Journal* columnist Jude Wanniski, the term was a deliberate swipe at prevailing Keynesian doctrines. Keynesians argued that corporate *demand* for new equipment gyrated through boom and bust cycles, disrupting jobs and economic stability. Governments needed to counteract this volatility by becoming stable sources of demand themselves, employing laid-off workers on public works programs or replacing lost wages with social insurance programs. Supply-siders, in contrast, contended that, if the economy failed to provide jobs for all, the fault lay in businesses' unwillingness to *supply* jobs in an economic climate poisoned by high taxes, unfair competition from government, and regulatory red-tape.

Reagan promised to "get government off our backs" by eliminating oppressive regulations and reducing tax rates. Within months of taking office in 1981, he signed the Kemp-Roth tax bill, slashing income taxes across the board—though the largest cuts by far accrued to the very rich. Reagan vowed to boost military spending and at the same time railed against the "out-of-control federal budget" and "runaway deficit of nearly $80 billion" run up by Democratic incumbent Jimmy Carter. In a major 1980 campaign speech, Reagan promised that, "Starting next year, the deficits will get smaller until in just a few years, the budget can be balanced. And we hope we can begin whittling away at that almost $1 trillion debt that hangs over the future of our children."[13]

Primary opponent George H. W. Bush derided Reagan's scheme as "voodoo economics" (at least until Reagan tapped him for the vice presidency) and Independent candidate John Anderson repeatedly challenged Reagan to explain, exactly, how he could cut taxes, raise military spending, and still balance the federal budget. It was soon evident that the numbers did not add up.

At Reagan's urging, Congress passed three major tax bills in the early 1980s, cutting taxes on the highest earners from 70 percent in 1980 to 28 percent by 1986.[14] The deficit swelled, tripling from $74 billion to $221 billion. Although the first Bush administration subsequently raised the top rate slightly—to 31 percent—this was not nearly enough to make a dent in the deficit. When George H. W. Bush stepped down in 1992, the federal government was borrowing $290 billion per year. During the twelve-year reign of Reagan-Bush, the annual deficit, the federal debt, and government's annual interest obligations all had quadrupled.

In 1981 Reagan's then—budget director David Stockman agreed to a series of interviews with the journalist William Greider and provided a remarkably candid commentary on the Machiavellian budget politics of the supply-siders. Stockman acknowledged that the administration's push for across-the-board tax cuts all along concealed its true agenda—to cut the tax rate on the highest incomes while curbing federal spending.

"The supply-side formula was the only way to get a tax

policy that was really 'trickle down,'" Stockman explained. "In order to make this palatable as a political matter you had to bring down all the brackets. . . . Kemp-Roth was always a Trojan horse to bring down the top rate." He described growing public alarm over deficits as "fortuitous" and was "buoyant" about the "tightening noose" the budgetary hole imposed on federal spending. Stockman, forced to resign after the interviews appeared in the *Atlantic*, went on to elucidate Reagan's strategy for dealing with the ballooning deficits: "Wage war with Congress over the budget issues and, in 1982, blame Democrats for whatever goes wrong."[15]

Much of the government's budget in the early 1980s was precommitted to fund entitlement programs like food stamps, Medicaid, veterans' benefits, Social Security pensions, and Medicare, whose costs rose inexorably with each uptick in the unemployment rate. Between mandated spending and the military buildup, overall federal spending did not slow at all during the Reagan-Bush years; relative to national output, federal spending from 1981 to 1992 grew to the highest levels attained in peacetime in the United States. But thanks to Reagan's war with the Democrats, growth in so-called discretionary spending—spending not mandated by existing law—ground to a halt.

Over the next two decades, virtually every proposal to enhance or even continue spending on discretionary social programs—from building new toilets in Yellowstone Park to expanding access to school-readiness programs for impoverished children—unleashed ferocious battles in Congress over the debt and the need to "tighten belts." Economists, backed by conservative think tanks like the Heritage Foundation and Cato Institute, called for balanced budgets to prevent inflation and bring down interest rates. That interest and inflation rates were falling throughout the 1980s, while the deficit soared, seemed to change nobody's mind. The economist Paul Krugman, one of many giving voice to such fears, called the 1990s an age of "diminished expectations," in which government, saddled with debt, would be unable to address the needs and demands of the electorate.[16] Corporate-sponsored advocacy organizations like the Concord Coalition made deficit reduction their mantra and overriding goal, sponsoring candidates, forums, and policy briefs on how best to balance the budget and live within the nation's means.

By the early 1990s, rampant deficit hysteria battered down remaining obstacles to budget cuts. Legal mandates no longer guaranteed protection. Congress looked for savings in veterans' programs, Social Security disability benefits, welfare spending, Medicaid and Medicare reimbursements, and student financial aid. Anyone who dared point out the obvious—that deficits would never have occurred without tax cuts, that if Congress was unwilling to tax the well-heeled, there was nothing to prevent it from borrowing their money, that deficit hysteria always centered, ultimately, on programs that redistributed the nation's income and ameliorated income disparities—was labeled "fiscally irresponsible." Conservatives shrewdly and purposefully seized upon the deficits to stalemate the legislative process and suppress political debate.

When Clinton took office in 1993 he found, according to the journalist Bob Woodward's account, that deficit politics presented a nearly insurmountable obstacle to any legislative agenda.[17] Under the tutelage of Treasury secretary and former Goldman Sachs chair Robert Rubin, Clinton's became the most fiscally conservative administration since Herbert Hoover.[18] In 1994 Republicans gained control of Congress and attempted to bury Keynesian stabilization policy by passing a constitutional amendment that would mandate an annually balanced federal budget. The amendment, which would have put an end once and for all to federal deficits and full-employment budgeting, failed passage in the Senate by one vote. Conservatives scored a partial victory, however, with the Balanced Budget Agreement of 1997, committing Congress and the administration to balance the budget each year for the next decade, regardless of the state of the economy—an agreement that hamstrung the Clinton administration but was promptly ignored by George W. Bush.

In 1998 the federal budget showed a surplus for the first time in thirty years. Clinton attributed the strong economy and roaring stock market to tough spending caps and fiscal restraint and pledged further fiscal austerity. White House press releases conceived the future exclusively in terms not simply of budgetary balance but of burgeoning surpluses and massive debt repayment. In his millennial State of the Union address, Clinton proposed to devote some $3.5 trillion in taxpayer revenue to debt repayment. Vice President Al Gore, campaigning for the presidency in 2000, assured voters that he planned to reduce the debt "even if the economy slows," and asserted that a recession would provide "an opportunity" to cut government spending "just like a corporation has to cut expenses if revenues fall."

When Democratic opponent Bill Bradley floated a modest proposal to use surplus funds for health care, Gore attacked the idea as "fiscally irresponsible," and warned it might plunge the U.S. economy into recession. Hillary Clinton, running for the Senate from New York in 2000, declared that most problems facing the country "cannot be solved by government" and staunchly supported running budget surpluses to pay off the national debt. Even during the brief period of federal budget surpluses and even among ostensible liberals, U.S. politics remained in the unrelenting grip of deficit politics.

George W. Bush's election tightened the screws. As with Reagan, Bush made an across-the-board tax cut the centerpiece of his campaign and, as with Reagan, the cuts—in taxes on dividends, capital gains, and inheritances as well as ordinary income—flowed primarily to those with incomes in the top 1 percent. The federal budget went from surplus to deficit within months. Bush's policies seemed cynically calculated to plunge the nation deeper into the morass of deficit politics, as conservatives gamely blamed the deficits on out-of-control federal spending and vowed to cut expenditures. By late 2003, as the annual deficit approached $500 billion, Democrats and Republicans traded jibes over who deserved the blame—Bush's tax cuts, Democrats' spending bills, or a hopelessly stalemated and recklessly out-of-control Congress. Few even bothered to suggest that the deficit might be a blessing for a rapidly deteriorating economy.

Deficit politics—the strident insistence that the budget be balanced and debt repaid—has hamstrung the American political system for decades, making it impossible to intelligently discuss the proper response of government to economic distress or to broach the topic of expanding federal programs. Supply-siders use tax cuts and the resulting deficits as a sly means to a larger end—shrinking the size and mandate of the federal government, shifting it away from the aim of promoting social welfare, and, by starving the Treasury of funds, eliminating the automatic growth in entitlement programs needed to mitigate market downturns and unemployment. Although both Reagan and George W. Bush insistently denied their tax cuts would cause deficits, deficits were the inevitable, indeed the desired, outcome.

Deficits make the job of federal retrenchment easier, providing a rationale to cut programs that the public supports. Calls for expanded child welfare, for well-funded education, for secure retirement and health care cannot be ignored completely, not when the government is flush with surplus funds. In times of deficits, though, they can be drowned out with sanctimonious speeches on the virtues of living within one's means, a lesson conservatives have learned well over the last twenty years. Conservatives have also learned that the austerity message finds a receptive audience in middle-class taxpayers forced to foot an ever larger share of the bill for government programs and suspicious of the loyalties of their elected officials.

The administration of George W. Bush, however, faced a political environment quite different from the 1980s. Conservatives, for one thing, apparently saw less need to disguise their intentions in a Trojan horse. In debate over the Bush tax bill, Bush frankly acknowledged that the cuts would spur "smaller government." Then–chief economic adviser R. Glenn Hubbard acknowledged, according to the *New York Times*, "that reducing the size of government was a goal of the deficit plan."[19] Liberal Democrats are less plainspoken. Congressional Democrats in recent years have wrapped themselves in the mantle of fiscal rectitude, opposing tax cuts not on the grounds that they are unfair, but on the grounds that they are fiscally reckless. Unwilling to engage conservatives in direct ideological debate over public priorities, liberals have painted themselves into a rhetorical corner and found themselves by 2003 in the uncomfortable position of opposing public borrowing to combat recession.

But deficit politics, with its confusing rhetoric, its cynical misrepresentations, its baffling contradictions, seems at last to have exhausted the American public. Polls show that Americans care little about the deficit but care greatly about retirement security, health care, and education. Perhaps American voters are itching for honest and meaningful debate about the proper role of government, what responsibility citizens bear for each other's welfare, and who should shoulder the costs.

Deficit politics also obscure the profound class stratification and ideological fissures of American political culture. Conventional wisdom, for example, holds that Wall

Street hates deficits; that bankers and investors, fearing the dreaded crowding-out effect, will bid down stock prices and drive up interest rates at the first whiff of a spike in federal borrowing. But recent history does not support this. Republicans have been responsible for the largest peacetime deficits ever seen, yet they invariably secure the lion's share of campaign funds and lobbying largesse from the finance industry.[20]

Under Republican leadership, deficits tend to redistribute wealth upward. Taxes are cut on the richest individuals and on corporations while spending beneficial to corporate interests—contracts for military hardware, export-import loans, agricultural subsidies—are quietly expanded.[21] The Treasury covers the budget shortfall by borrowing on financial markets, primarily from wealthy individuals and financial institutions, who loan the money to cover the deficits that their tax breaks and expanded subsidies created, and then are paid interest on the funds they lent.

Congress, meanwhile, erupts in wrath over "out-of-control entitlements" and proposes "painful but essential" cuts in social insurance—food stamps, Medicaid, disability insurance, school lunch and child nutrition programs, legal aid, college grants, job-training programs, family welfare programs. The wealthy do not fund candidates promising upper-income tax cuts simply to have their wealth redistributed in any case via deficit-financed social programs. Cuts in social programs are the whole point of the game.

Democratic administrations, on the other hand, receive

zero indulgence toward deficits. When suspected liberals hold power, no degree of fiscal prudence appears sufficient to placate financial markets. This was exceedingly clear during the Clinton years. In 1993, with Democrats still in control of Congress, Clinton supported legislation that raised the top marginal tax rate to 39.6 percent; by any standard of fiscal responsibility, an eminently prudent action. Convinced by economists that budgetary virtue would be rewarded with lower interest rates and growth in the private economy, Clinton set about to cut waste in the bloated defense budget, slicing it by nearly a quarter during his eight-year tenure. Expansion of health and welfare programs was relegated to the back burner, not tossed aside. In fact, once the deficit began shrinking, Clinton pushed through a sizable expansion of the earned-income tax credit—a subsidy to low-wage workers and their families—and proposed plans to commit substantial federal revenues to the aged. Mindful of Wall Street's presumed hostility to deficits, though, he insisted that all plans were contingent upon continued improvement in the budget picture.

This earned him no respite whatsoever. Not only did interest rates not fall, as predicted, but conservative Republicans, having gained control of the House and Senate in 1994 under the leadership of House Speaker Newt Gingrich, lambasted Clinton with renewed vigor as a "tax and spend" Democrat.[22] In 1996 congressional conservatives pressed on with efforts to cut social spending and balance the budget. Cornered, the Clinton administration acquiesced to the

1997 Balanced Budget Agreement and pushed through large cuts in welfare spending.

The wealthy do not oppose deficits, per se. They understand, rather, that Keynesian policies are redistributive both in impact and intent. The very argument for fiscal-stabilization policy and deficit spending rests on a belief that market economies, for all their dynamism and successes, are deeply flawed, susceptible to periodic crises that needlessly endanger the livelihoods and security of the citizenry. New Deal liberals held the unemployed blameless for their plight and urged governments to use their unique financial resources to relieve economic distress.

Keynes understood that matters of debt and budget deficits, of interest payments and paper wealth that so obsess private businesspeople and financial interests, are, ultimately, irrelevant to all but the wealthy elite. The central insight of Keynesian thought was that real wealth lies in the people, resources, and productive apparatus of a society and that citizens can, through the collective power of government, harness those resources for internal development and security.

U.S. liberals are reluctant to acknowledge this frankly, but business interests are not fooled by their reticence. Conservative organizations fully appreciate the critique of business implicit in Keynesian thought and remain hostile to Keynesian policy.

The finance industry's hostility to government economic management was manifested very clearly by the Moody bond-rating agency's 2002 decision to downgrade Japanese government debt. Moody's ranking, which rates securities issued by the Japanese treasury below those of impoverished Botswana, is an undisguised attack on Japan's vigorous use of deficit spending to alleviate unemployment during a nearly decade-long economic slump. Stabilization efforts substantially increased Japan's public debt—all of which is denominated in yen and virtually all of it held by the Japanese public. Thanks to state spending, the Japanese unemployment rate remains below 6 percent despite a prolonged slump, and wages over the decade have remained stable. As with U.S. debt, default is unthinkable and would unleash a political crisis, destroying confidence in the yen. Moody's action is an unmistakable signal of the financial industry's extreme displeasure with governments that attempt to meddle in the marketplace.[23]

Financial censure of socialistic state policies extends to wealthy European nations as well. In the early 1990s financial institutions, unhappy with the social democratic policies and high taxes commonplace in northern and central Europe, dumped public bonds and bid down the value of national currencies. Under pressure from business interests, a dozen European governments entered into the Maastricht agreement, committing themselves to fiscal austerity and sharply restricted public-sector borrowing. Today, the European Union's Stability and Growth Pact limits annual national deficits in each of the participating countries to 3 percent of a nation's GDP—a level, even the conservative *Economist* magazine admits, is inadequate to combat a run-of-the-mill recession, never mind jobless rates that reached 10 percent in Germany in 2003. An article that year in *Business Week* pointed out that, because of the new fiscal restrictions, Germany, once looked to as the "locomotive of Western Europe," is now "reliant on other countries for most of its growth."[24]

The International Monetary Fund, increasingly regarded as a voice for financial interests throughout the world, routinely requires fiscal austerity plans from developing countries as a condition for receiving loans.[25] The financial community's insistence that developing countries balance their national budgets has killed efforts to spur internal growth through public spending programs. In an article on the downgrade in Japan's bond-rating, the *New York Times* pointed out that Botswana has a public sector debt equal to a mere 10 percent of its GDP. The authors do not point out that the population of Botswana, decimated by AIDS, might be better off had their government utilized more of the country's resources on their behalf.

THE MYTH OF THE SOCIAL SECURITY TRUST FUND

Of the approximately $2.7 trillion in federal bonds held in government accounts, half sit in the Social Security Trust Fund. These bonds represent the one potentially burdensome obligation the government faces, since, unlike other public debts, the government may one day need to repay

Social Security out of current tax revenues. Paradoxically, the debt to Social Security is the liability that politicians are most likely to minimize.

From its inception in 1935, Social Security funds came from a dedicated tax on wages and salaries. Wages up to $87,000 are taxed at 12.4 percent, half paid by employees and half by the employer.[26] Earnings above $87,000 are not taxed, nor is income from interest and dividends, making the payroll tax a frankly regressive levy. Economists label Social Security a "pay-as-you-go" system, because funds collected in a given year were typically paid out to beneficiaries, not saved and invested on behalf of future retirees—the program was not "prefunded."

In the 1980s, however, the Social Security Administration (SSA) began to collect more payroll taxes than it paid out in pension, survivor, and disability benefits each year. The difference between receipts and outlays grew through the 1990s, and now amounts to some $160 billion each year. Social Security expects to continue running annual surpluses at least through 2020. Each year, the SSA turns any surplus funds over to the U.S. Treasury, which spends them. In return, SSA receives U.S. Treasury securities, representing an implicit promise by the U.S. government to repay Social Security when and if additional money is needed to cover benefits. These bonds are what we call the "Trust Fund." In 2003 the Trust Fund contained bonds valued at about $1.4 trillion; by 2020 the accumulated surpluses should approach $4 trillion.

This, of course, is a projection—the surpluses could be

larger or smaller than anticipated, depending on wage growth, population changes, the overall state of the economy, and so on. Under the SSA's best-case scenario the Social Security trust fund will grow continuously throughout the twenty-first century—reaching as much as $18 trillion in 2080. Under its worst-case scenario, the fund will run out in 2031.

What is the purpose of all this "saving up"? Ostensibly, we are saving for the baby-boom generation, whose members will soon begin retiring. Since American women are having fewer children and retirees are living longer, the ratio of retired people to working adults will undoubtedly rise as the boomers age and, unless our future workers are more productive than the SSA predicts (and they may well be) supporting all these retirees could cost more than 12.4 percent of their wages.

SSA's economic forecasts have been fairly glum. Its intermediate-case scenario, most widely cited by commentators, forecasts that Social Security will collect ample revenue from payroll taxes alone to pay all benefits until 2017. For ten years after that, payroll taxes plus the interest Treasury pays on the Trust Fund's bonds will cover all benefits. After this, SSA will need to redeem (or cash in) the bonds. When that happens, the system will have enough revenue—from payroll taxes, interest, and bond redemptions—to pay legislated benefits for another fifteen years.

If and when payroll tax receipts fall below projected benefit payments—once the SSA actually needs the interest and principle from the bonds to meet its obligations—the federal government will have to find resources to pay the SSA, just like it has to find resources to pay back any other creditor. Congress can obtain the cash by raising taxes, cutting spending on other federal programs, or borrowing funds from the financial markets. Unlike other financial obligations of the government, this debt cannot simply be "rolled over." Retirees will need an actual stream of income—a valid and reliable claim on the economy's output. Liberals, who support Social Security and tend to minimize potential problems, contend that the system has enough money to last through 2042 when all the bonds are redeemed—which as purely an accounting matter is correct. Conservatives, who dislike Social Security and tend to exaggerate flaws, argue that the system will be in trouble in 2017, once payroll taxes fall below outlays—which as a practical matter of federal budgeting is also correct.

The political debate is confusing because saving up for Social Security never made any economic sense. The federal government collects excess payroll taxes, spends all surpluses, and replaces them with bonds. These are special-issue, nonnegotiable bonds and cannot be redeemed for cash unless Congress specifically allocates money for their redemption. If future Congresses choose not to repay Social Security, they can simply raise payroll taxes or cut pension benefits. The bonds in the Trust Fund are simply an accounting entry denoting the magnitude of the public's commitment to future retirees, which the public may or may not choose to honor.

The idea of "saving" for the baby-boomer retirement

originated with the Reagan administration in the 1980s. At the time, the Trust Fund was sold as a method for prefunding the impending baby-boom retirement; in fact the excess payroll taxes combined with sharp cuts in top income tax rates shifted much of the federal tax burden from the wealthy to wage earners with moderate incomes. Trust Fund surpluses, small at first, were barely noticed in the deluge of red ink from the Reagan-Bush era. Today, however, over one-quarter of federal revenues derive from the payroll tax, one of the most regressive of federal taxes. Of this money, about one-fifth is surplus, not needed to pay current Social Security benefits. It is credited to the Trust Fund, but is destined, in fact, for general government spending.

Many Democrats argue that this elaborate accounting chimera provides Social Security with a veneer of fiscal planning that defuses right-wing attacks on the system. By creating an illusion of prefunding, the Trust Fund instills confidence among voters that their benefits are "paid up" and hence secure.

President Clinton bound Democrats securely to the Trust Fund when he proposed in 1998 that Social Security's surpluses be used exclusively to repay other federal debts. How the Treasury uses surplus Social Security funds— whether to repay debt, increase spending, cut other taxes— makes absolutely no difference to Social Security. SSA receives the same number of bonds in any case. But Clinton shrewdly calculated that, if he could maneuver congressional Republicans into an agreement to "save" the surpluses in a rhetorical "lockbox," he would thwart efforts to give the funds away as tax cuts. Politically, Clinton turned the tables on the Republican Party, presenting the Democrats both as the guardians of Social Security and as upholders of fiscal virtue.

Conservatives were not taken in. They are well aware that Social Security's bonds represent a promise to the aged that society will one day be asked to keep. Most oppose higher taxes, have little faith in the ability of government to cut spending, and object on principle to federal borrowing for social programs. Business lobbyists resent the payroll tax and many are none too keen on the idea of American workers retiring into extended periods of idleness. In the 1930s when Social Security was established, conservative business groups vehemently opposed it. They gave their support grudgingly, and only when then-president Roosevelt assured them that the system would be funded entirely by payroll taxes on workers. General income taxes, paid largely by upper-income groups, were never to be tapped for Social Security.

But if governments of the future are to honor the commitment implicit in the Trust Fund, general revenues will have to be tapped. If the SSA's pessimistic projections prove correct, real resources will need to be transferred to retirees, above and beyond the 12.4 percent payroll tax, so that retirees can survive without a paycheck. The amount needed is not large, but it is large enough to worry those corporate and wealthy taxpayers who neither want nor need Social Security and who are likely to be asked to foot the bill.

The National Association of Manufacturers, concerned

that its members' profits might be targeted, has endorsed privatization of Social Security—replacing the pay-as-you-go transfer program with individually owned savings accounts—to foreclose the establishment of an uncontrolled "baby boomer entitlement."[27] The *Wall Street Journal* columnist Alan Murray wrote ominously of the "aging baby-boomer assault on the federal budget" and the threat that "general revenues," rather than payroll taxes, may one day be tapped to pay benefits.[28] The libertarian economist Milton Friedman proposed in the *New York Times* that the Trust Fund be liquidated and the Social Security system disbanded.[29] The libertarian Cato Institute and conservative Heritage Foundation have poured millions into promoting privatization schemes. Upon taking office, the Bush administration immediately appointed a presidential commission, heavy with Cato and Heritage staffers, to devise plans for privatizing Social Security, and the commission dutifully began its report with the claim that the system is "not sustainable as currently structured."[30]

But private savings accounts—the Bush commission's alternative—cannot solve the potential problem of the baby-boomer retirement. The growing ranks of seniors will need a reliable claim on the output of younger generations, and private accounts like 401(k)s promise a claim on nothing in particular. The bonds in the Trust Fund do represent a potential claim by SSA on future federal revenues, yet that claim would exist with or without the bonds. The Social Security Trust Fund was designed to solve a potential economic problem—transferring resources to seniors in the

future so that American workers can continue to enjoy retirement—with a political accounting device. Today, privatization boosters are exploiting the contradictions inherent
in that accounting device to attack Social Security and to
justify regressive policies like raising the retirement age,
shaving cost-of-living adjustments, or otherwise cutting
retirement benefits.

Liberal political analysts today complain openly that the
binds tying Democrats to the Trust Fund surpluses are fast
becoming the rope with which the party will hang itself.
Writing in the liberal *American Prospect*, Robert Borosage
excoriates the Democrats for promoting fiscal belt-tighten-
ing.[31] The columnist Robert Kuttner worries that "many
Democrats are taking surplus-worship to such an extreme
that they are in danger of losing their raison d'être as a party."

"Conservative Democrats," Kuttner writes, "are determined to expunge the Democrats' legacy as the party of 'tax
and spend.' The trouble is, the Democrats' signature programs are nothing if not tax and spend. Social Security raises
trillions of dollars in payroll taxes and spends the money on
secure retirement. Medicare, likewise, is tax and spend. So
is public education. As a party, you can't make your centerpiece the defense of Social Security and Medicare, much less
the addition of prescription-drug benefits or enriched
child-care programs if you use 'tax and spend' as an epithet.
Surplus-worship makes it even harder to remain the party
of public improvement."[32]

In his scathing assessment of the Clinton administration, *No One Left to Lie To*, the journalist Christopher Hitch-

ens coined the term "triangulation" to describe Clinton's penchant for transforming conservative causes into Democratic platform planks.[33] Hitchens focused on Clinton's foreign and domestic policy initiatives. But triangulation also captures Clinton's use of the Social Security and federal budget politics to deflect conservative attacks while maneuvering the Democratic Party to the right. The rhetoric of the Trust Fund—of saving up, balanced budgets, fiscal responsibility, and debt repayment, has made liberals and conservatives alike complicit in the effort to mislead the public and misrepresent the nature of federal debts.

The nation's elderly and aging boomers do not need a Trust Fund. Nor do they need an expanded system of private savings accounts. What they need is a firm commitment by the public to provide for them in their old age. In return, they should make a commitment of their own: to invest directly in the well-being of the nation's children, whose future is the only trust fund we can depend upon.

THE PARADOX OF THRIFT

Savings and *investment* are perhaps the two most misunderstood and misused words in the English vocabulary. According to the dictionary, *save* means "to accumulate money," while *invest* means "to commit money or capital in order to gain a financial return." Colloquially, saving is putting aside money and investing is what one does with the money put aside. But economists use these terms differently and the differences are critical to understanding the ways in which the financialization of U.S. economic discourse skews our policy priorities.

To economists, "savings" refers to income generated in a given year that is not used by households to purchase goods and services produced in that year. To save, therefore is to "not spend" on currently produced output. This can encompass many acts besides accumulating money. Buying a used car, purchasing real estate, "investing" in the stock market or gold or rare coins would all count, in economic data, as acts of saving. Income not spent on the goods and services produced by the economy is income that was generated by the economy's production, but did not return to the economy in the form of demand for the output the economy produced.

Savings is most usefully envisaged as a physical concept. Each year businesses turn out automobiles, computers, lumber, and refrigerators. Households (or consumers) buy most, but not all, of this output for their homes. The computers and cars they leave behind represent the economy's savings. Economics students are encouraged to visualize the economy as a metaphorical plumbing system through which goods and money flow. Firms produce goods, which flow through the marketplace and are converted into money. The money flows into peoples' pockets as income, which flows back into the marketplace as demand for output. Savings represent a leak in the plumbing and can upset the economy's stability. If other purchasers don't step up and buy the output that consumers have left behind, the economy will go into recession. Firms will lay off workers and curb production, for there is no profit in making goods that people don't want to buy.

On the other hand, the stuff consumers decline to buy is available for businesses to purchase in order to expand their capacity or upgrade their technology. When banks buy computers, when livery services buy automobiles, or developers buy lumber and appliances, then the excess goods find a market and production continues apace. Economists refer to business purchases of new plant and equipment as "investment." In the plumbing metaphor, investment is conceived of as an injection—an additional flow of spending into the economy to offset the leaks caused by household saving.

The plumbing metaphor can be extended to encompass other sectors. Imports (spending income on goods not made in one's own country) cause leaks, which can be offset by exports (foreigners spending their income on goods produced in our country). Taxes—income paid to the government and no longer available for consumers to spend—are hopefully counteracted by the government's own spending (unless of course the government runs a budget surplus and itself becomes a source of saving).

When monetary market economies developed in Europe in the 1800s, high rates of unemployment and low wages ensured that about probably no more than half of all income flowed to consumers. Business owners retained most of the rest as profit.[34] As an accounting matter, this meant that a substantial fraction of income was saved (not spent by consumers). Economic commentators at the time held this to be a good thing. If workers received all the economy's income, writers like Thomas Malthus argued at the turn of the nineteenth century, they would fritter it away on large families. Low wages and correspondingly high levels of saving ensured that business owners commanded a sizable portion of the economy's output for new investment and new investment—plant, equipment, technological advances—raised productivity and fostered economic growth. In the early years of capitalist development, rapid innovation and fierce competition did indeed compel business owners to spend their profits on expansion, rather than becoming savers themselves.

By the turn of the twentieth century, however, high saving rates had become a drag on economic growth. Small entrepreneurial businesses gave way to immense monopolistic firms like U.S. Steel and Standard Oil, whose profits vastly exceeded what they could spend on expansion. Indeed, expansion often looked pointless since, given the low level of wages and household spending, the only buyers for their output were other businesses, which themselves faced the same dilemma. As market economies matured, savings became a source not of growth but of economic stagnation. Even the lavish personal spending of business owners and their shareholders could not provide enough demand to purchase the output churned out each year in large industrial factories. Henry Ford was the first American corporate leader to deliberately pay his workers above-market wages, reasoning correctly that a better-paid work force would provide the only reliable market for his automobiles.[35]

Today, at the turn of the twenty-first century, the United

States and other industrialized countries are even more mature and the need for continued high levels of business investment is less obvious. Thanks to democratic suffrage, labor unions, social welfare programs, and a generally more egalitarian culture, wages are far higher in developed economies than they were a century ago; wage and salary earners now secure from 70 to 80 percent of national income. And households spend most of what they earn. This leaves less of the economy's output behind for new investment, but it also ensures that output produced finds a market and continues to be produced.

The personal savings rate in the United States—the percentage of income flowing to households that they do not spend—fell to 1 percent in the late 1990s. Today, as a stagnant economy makes consumers more cautious, the personal savings rate is around 4 percent.

Is this a bad thing? Listening to many conservative economists and politicians, one would think it is. Americans are often chastised for their lack of thrift, their failure to provide for themselves financially, their rash and excessive borrowing, their dependence on government for big-ticket items they ought to provide for themselves. Politicians and economists often argue that Americans need to save more and have devised numerous schemes to induce them to do so—medical savings accounts, college savings accounts, retirement savings accounts, dependent-care accounts. Americans are urged to save in more subtle ways as well. When legislators cut or threaten to cut unemployment, health and Social Security benefits, or student financial aid, people are spurred to save more. Proposals to weaken consumer bankruptcy protections encourage people to save up for big purchases instead of borrowing.

Yet Americans are also constantly exhorted to spend. After September 11, President Bush told the public they could best serve their country by continuing to shop. In the media, economic experts bemoan declines in "consumer confidence" and applaud reports of buoyant retail or auto sales. The U.S. economy, we are told, is a consumer economy; our spendthrift ways and shop-till-you-drop culture the motor that propels us. Free-spending consumers armed with multiple credit cards keep the stores hopping, the restaurants full, and the factories humming. Business investment is important as well, but investment trends can be erratic; technology or construction booms often precede busts. Consumer spending is more reliable.

The entire economic system demands that people spend freely—there would be no point in employing people to churn out endless streams of goods and services each year if people did not buy them. Yet the U.S. political system compels individuals to save, or at least to try and save.

Our schizophrenic outlook on saving and spending has two roots. First, the idea of saving meshes seamlessly with a conservative ideological outlook. In what the author George Lakoff calls the "strict-father morality" that informs conservative Republican politics, abstinence, thrift, self-reliance, and competitive individualism are moral virtues and an economic system that rewards success and punishes failure encourages people to act morally.[36] Saving, from this perspective, promotes abstinence and self-reliance. Institutions that discourage saving—like Social Security, unemployment insurance, government health programs, state-funded student aid—are by definition socialistic and result in an immoral reliance on others. Former Treasury secretary Paul O'Neill bluntly expressed this idea to a reporter for the *Financial Times* in 2001. "Able-bodied adults," O'Neill opined, "should save enough on a regular basis so that they can provide for their own retirement and for that matter for their health and medical needs." Otherwise, he continued, elderly people are just "dumping their problems on the broader society."[37]

This ideological position, which is widely but not deeply shared among U.S. voters, receives financial and political support from the finance industry. Economists may not define savings as "accumulating money," but accumulating money is the predictable result of not spending. And while economists might not define investment as "committing money to gain a financial return," the finance industry sees investment this way and in fact, specializes in committing accumulated pools of money to the purchase of stocks, bonds, and other paper assets, for which it receives generous fees and commissions.

Financial firms have funded most of the research, advertising, lobbying, and public relations for the campaign to "privatize" Social Security, replacing the pay-as-you-go system with individual investment accounts. Secretary O'Neill's reflections on savings came as he was preparing to address the Coalition for American Financial Security, a group composed largely of financial-services firms committed to partial privatization of Social Security—reportedly to raise $20 million for an advertising blitz in support of privatization.[38] Along with the Universal Savers Alliance and the Cato Institute, the coalition has been a primary source of advocacy for private accounts. Privatization supporters have also enlisted conservative economists to their cause who—harking back to the conventional wisdom of the 1800s—maintain that private accounts will spur growth by "increasing national savings."[39]

The finance industry and its wealthy clients also advocate "consumption taxes"—levying taxes on income spent, but not on income saved, so as to "encourage saving" and "reward thrift." Indeed, the Bush Treasury Department was in 2003 reportedly considering proposals "scrapping the current income tax" in favor of a national sales or value-added tax.[40]

Heavy lobbying by financial firms also propelled recent legislation making it difficult for consumers to wipe out debts. Drafted with input from lawyers and lobbyists for banks and credit card companies, the bankruptcy bill's progress through Congress was smoothed by generous campaign contributions. Finance and credit card companies quintupled their campaign donations during the 1990s. MBNA, the world's largest credit-card issuer, gave $3.5 million in 2000, 86 percent of it to Republican candidates, according to the Center for Responsive Politics. The bill was expected to increase the yearly profits of MNBA alone by $75 million.[41]

Fortunately for the U.S. economy, political pressures for higher saving have not translated into much actual saving. Wealthy households of course save. Affidavits filed during his divorce proceedings revealed that Jack Welch receives a monthly retirement income of $1.4 million but has monthly expenditures of only $366,114 of it—for a personal savings rate of 74 percent.[42] Growing inequality of income distribution in the United States, however, generates a high demand for the millions that wealthy individuals like Welch set aside each month. Much of the savings of people like Welch are funneled through the financial system and recycled in the form of consumer borrowing. Indeed, consumer debt loads increased two or three times as fast as household income during the 1990s. Debt service now eats up nearly one-quarter of the typical household's income. And despite a rapid escalation in housing prices, Americans—thanks to home-equity loans and cash-out refinancings—had less home equity in 2001 than they did a decade ago.[43]

Consumer borrowing fuels consumer spending, which keeps the economy chugging. But borrowing also makes consumers anxious about their ability to repay or continue borrowing should they lose a job. When growth is fed by borrowing, the economy is less stable than if income were simply distributed more equitably and spending supported by dependable social assistance programs. One of the strongest inducements to save is the feeling that we have nobody to rely upon in adversity but ourselves. Threats to health care benefits, to social security, to public support for higher education, unemployment insurance, and bankruptcy protections may one day result in substantially higher rates of saving. If that day comes, the United States may find itself trapped, like Japan, in an endless slump in which insecure households, forced to save against old age and hard times, succeed in bringing those hard times upon us.

CHAPTER FOUR

THE INFLATION MYTH

Several years ago, the Yale economist Robert Shiller conducted a survey of public attitudes toward inflation. He queried people in the United States, Germany, and Brazil—countries with very different experiences of inflation—and further categorized respondents by age to assess whether having lived through a period of high inflation altered people's views. In all age groups and in all three countries, overwhelming majorities fully agreed that controlling inflation "is an important national priority," as important as "preventing drug abuse or deterioration in the quality of our schools." Respondents expressed virtually unanimous agreement that inflation "reduces the growth and economic progress of a country" and that "if inflation ever gets started," there is a risk of it getting "out of control," which "can lead to political and economic chaos." Survey respondents not only concurred that controlling inflation is "one of the most important missions of economic policy," but three in four supported fighting inflation even if this "would result in an unemployment rate of 9 percent."

When asked to explain their views, people felt that "millions, like me, would be forced into poverty" and "forced to seek assistance" because of inflation. Respondents worried that because of inflation "the economy would collapse"; "we wouldn't be able to afford anything"; and "the gap between the rich and the poor will become so great there will no longer be a middle income group or even the potential of one."

Shiller carried out the surveys in the mid-1990s, a period when inflation had been low and falling in almost all countries. Yet media commentators invoked the term *inflation* constantly when discussing the economy—50 percent more often than they referred to unemployment, though unemployment rose markedly in the 1980s and remained stubbornly high through the mid-1990s. Shiller speculated that the public anxieties about the economy in general had become bound up with the idea of inflation.[1] Inflation, for example, is a prime component of the so-called misery index—a term coined by the conservative economist Robert Barro and popularized by President Reagan. The sum of the unemployment rate and the inflation rate, the misery index was widely cited as a bellwether of economic performance. During the 1980s, when unemployment reached levels not seen since the Great Depression, the misery index fell sharply as rising unemployment was offset by markedly lower inflation.

With inflation so widely invoked as a source of distress, it is little wonder that Shiller found such widespread public aversion toward it. Yet this antipathy is misplaced. Not only is inflation not as harmful as people presume, the dire economic effects people attribute to inflation are in fact likely to result from efforts to fight inflation. To prevent prices from rising periodically in minimally regulated market economies, growth must be suppressed and demands for higher wages resisted. But policies explicitly aimed at curtailing growth in jobs and incomes will almost certainly be rejected by voters in democratic societies. In the 1980s and 1990s inflation policy was ceded to central banks like the U.S. Federal Reserve, which, insulated from politics and cloaked in the mystique of complex financial jargon, implemented programs that would never have passed muster in the political arena.

SOME DEFINITIONS

Inflation—An increase in the average level of prices, measured as a positive increase in the consumer price index (CPI).

Consumer price index—An index that measures the average cost of purchasing a bundle of goods and services that typifies the standard of living of the average U.S. urban household.

Accelerating inflation—A situation in which the rate of inflation is increasing over time.

Disinflation—A situation in which, though prices are rising on average, the rate of inflation is declining over time.

Deflation—A decrease in the average level of prices.

Hyperinflation—A situation in which there is very high and rapidly accelerating inflation. Although there is no official definition—no

specific level at which ordinary inflation becomes hyperinflation—generally, when prices rise at annual rates much above 40
percent, this is regarded as hyperinflation.

Nominal income—The stated, dollar value of one's income (wage,
salary, or price).

Real income—The nominal value of one's income adjusted for
inflation—that is, the value of one's income relative to the average
prices of goods and services or the purchasing power of a given
money income.

Nominal interest rate—The stated, numerical interest rate charged
on a loan contract.

Real interest rate—The nominal interest rate adjusted for inflation.
This can be found by subtracting the inflation rate from the nominal interest rate.

Fed Funds rate—The interest rate banks charge one another for
very-short-term (often overnight) loans of their cash reserves.

Central bank—The body responsible for printing currency and setting monetary policy.

Monetary policy—Policies that determine the cost and availability
of money and credit in the economy.

Federal Reserve—The name of the U.S. central bank.

WHAT'S WRONG WITH INFLATION?

It has become an article of faith in the mainstream media
that inflation—a rise in the average level of prices—is destructive and that any and all tools should be used to combat
it. To drive the point home, financial writers often use me-

chanical metaphors. Economies are said to "run too hot" or to "overheat." Inflation is signified by a train careening out of control. To prevent "runaway" inflation, we need to "tap the brakes" and "cool down" the economic "engine." When the Federal Reserve, throughout the late 1990s, warned repeatedly of "inflationary forces that could undermine economic growth," neither media commentators nor politicians questioned the presumption that inflation wreaks economic havoc.

Yet neither history nor logic supports this view. Gradually rising prices are endemic to market economies. After World War II, the governments of virtually all developed and most of the less-developed countries adopted policies intended to promote growth and high levels of employment. The consequence of steady and stable growth, it was widely understood, would be steady and even rising inflation. In a country that utilizes most of its resources most of the time, neither workers nor small businesses nor large corporations will face competitive pressures to accept wage cuts or slash prices. Human nature being what it is, most will instead try to raise their prices, and the result, inevitably, is a rise in the average level of prices.

In 1958 the British economist A. W. Phillips pointed out that nominal wages (wages in money terms, unadjusted for changes in prices) consistently rose when unemployment fell and fell when unemployment rose. Phillips's data was limited to the experience of the United Kingdom, but his findings were soon generalized to all market economies. Low unemployment means rising wages, and rising wages, when passed along in the prices of goods and services, result in higher rates of inflation.[2] Low inflation correlated with higher unemployment, across countries and over time.

The "Phillips Curve" set off a debate in policy circles about the costs of preventing or reducing inflation. The costs of unemployment are well known. Unemployed workers translate into lost output and income for the economy as a whole. Arthur Okun, chair of the President's Council of Economic Advisers under Lyndon Johnson, estimated that a 1 percent uptick in U.S. unemployment resulted in a 3 percent loss of output—the goods and services those unemployed workers might otherwise have produced. For those without jobs, unemployment means poverty, insecurity, depression, and family stress. For society, higher unemployment equals more crime, suicide, drug abuse, and domestic violence.

But what are the costs of inflation? As Shiller's survey makes clear, most people equate inflation with a deteriorating standard of living. But this is not obvious. Inflation involves a rise in the level of prices overall—not simply an increase in the prices of a few items like health insurance or college tuition—and thus an increase in the "cost of living." But when considered from the perspective of the economy as a whole, prices are merely the flip side of income—the ten dollars you pay for a movie ticket is ultimately distributed among the public as wages, profits, interest, and dividends. Higher prices in general therefore translate into higher incomes. The monetary cost of purchasing goods and services rises with inflation, but so too do the money incomes available to make purchases.

For the typical person, the question is not whether prices are increasing, but whether prices are rising by more or less than one's own income. Workers in high demand—skilled workers, professionals, or anyone working in a field where jobs are plentiful and business is buoyant—can generally "keep up" with inflation, negotiating wage increases that keep abreast of rising price levels.

In inflationary periods, workers protected by unions typically negotiate annual "cost-of-living adjustments" as part of their contracts. Social Security pensions are adjusted each year to compensate for rising prices. Large businesses with some pricing power protect their incomes by passing higher costs to consumers. But small businesses often fare well in inflationary environments as well. The problem, of course, is that nobody knows for sure whether his or her own income will keep up with price hikes, so the prospect of rising costs makes people understandably anxious and uncertain of their own prospects.

On the other hand, it is impossible to be certain that one's income will keep up even when prices are not rising or, for that matter, when prices are falling. The most powerful determinant of whether wages and salaries rise, fall, or remain stable in real terms—that is, in terms of their purchasing power, after adjusting for inflation—is not the inflation rate but the unemployment rate. Holding on to one's job and living standard is a struggle in the best of circumstances; it is not necessarily more difficult when prices are rising.

There is evidence that some employers, worried about employee morale, are reluctant to cut the nominal salaries of current employees. In this case, inflation enables them to cut wages on the sly, simply by granting raises too small to meet the rise in prices. If prices rise by 4 percent and you receive only a 2 percent raise, you are 2 percent worse off. But other firms do cut wages in a downturn; many achieve sizable pay cuts by laying off existing employees and replacing them with lower-paid contractors.[3] This strategy is more common when unemployment is high and jobs are scarce. If your wage falls by 2 percent when inflation is zero, you are still 2 percent worse off. All in all, the typical wage or salary earner will likely fare better when prices are rising than when they are stable or falling, simply because inflation is so often associated with low unemployment rates. Evidence abounds that countries willing to tolerate moderate inflation are able to sustain higher rates of job growth for longer periods of time. A study by economists at the World Bank found that inflation rates of up to 20 percent annually are correlated, throughout the world, with higher rates of economic growth.[4]

The economist Justin Wolfers looked at surveys conducted in numerous countries that asked people to rank their general level of satisfaction with their lives. Rising inflation rates had virtually no impact on the proportion of people who declared themselves "very satisfied." Rising unemployment rates, though, caused satisfaction levels to drop precipitously.[5]

If there is a trade-off between jobs and growth on the one hand and stable prices on the other and if the social costs of joblessness are very high, then what exactly is the argument for stable prices? Are there costs to inflation that need to be considered as well?

Because inflation raises incomes along with prices, economists have tried to identify social costs caused specifically by inflation—costs imposed by inflation alone rather than by the declines in income or living standards that might occur with or without inflation. They have identified only one significant negative consequence: inflation erodes the value of money over time.

For anyone who earns money in the form of an annual income, this is not a concern, since incomes rise along with inflation. But for those who live on accumulated financial wealth or whose income is locked in by a long-term contract, inflation is insidiously destructive. The value of a fixed sum of money deteriorates each year by the rate of inflation, eating away wealth and living standards. Two distinct demographic groups fall into this category. First are retirees dependent on past savings or on private pensions. Second, fewer in number but far more consequential politically, is a group sometimes referred to as rentiers—individuals and institutions with substantial accumulated wealth who live on the interest income generated by financial assets—banks, financial firms, and their wealthy clients.

Rentiers try to protect their wealth from inflation by incorporating an expected "inflation premium" into the interest rate they charge when lending their money. If inflation is running, for example, at 2 percent each year and rentiers want real (inflation-adjusted) interest earnings of 4 percent, they will charge 6 percent interest on loans—a 4 percent real return plus 2 percent to cover the rate at which their money is losing value each year. However, bonds and other loan contracts are often written for very long periods—ten, twenty, or thirty years. Interest is fixed when the contract is written, but inflation can change dramatically. A period of accelerating inflation will wear away the real value of the interest and, if prices rise fast enough, eat into the principle itself.

In the early 1960s, U.S. lenders underwrote thirty-year corporate bonds and home mortgages at interest rates ranging from 4 to 6 percent, while inflation averaged 1 to 3 percent. In 1969 the inflation rate reached 6 percent. By 1979, the inflation rate spiked at 13 percent. As inflation crept steadily upward, the real value of these old loans plummeted. Furthermore, thanks to heavy competition and federal restrictions on interest rates, lenders found it difficult to charge enough interest on new loans to offset rising inflation. Real returns on lending fell below zero. By 1979, the real interest rate on new home mortgages fell to negative 3 percent—the interest lenders received failed to compensate them for the decline in the purchasing power of their money. In terms of real goods and services, borrowers were paying back less, even with interest factored in, than they had borrowed.

For heavily indebted middle-class families, inflation was a positive godsend. It lifted the monetary value of their incomes and their homes, while whittling away the real burden of their mortgages, student loans, and credit card balances. But for financial firms and the wealthy clients who financed them, rising inflation spelled disaster. The distribution of wealth in the United States shifted dramatically. The economist Edward Wolff estimates that in the early

1960s, the richest 1 percent commanded one-third of all household wealth. By the end of the 1970s, as debtors repaid loans in debased currency, their share of household wealth had fallen to one-fifth.[6]

Inflation, as any economics textbook will teach, redistributes income and wealth from creditors to debtors. Thus it harms mostly the well-heeled minority who control most financial assets. Disinflation, on the other hand—a decline in the inflation rate—enriches creditors at the expense of debtors who contracted for loans at interest rates established when inflation was higher. During the disinflationary period of 1980–2000, wealth distribution reverted back to prewar patterns. By 2000, Wolff estimates, the richest 1 percent controlled 40 percent of all financial wealth.

But the most widespread damage is caused by deflation, an actual decline in the general level of prices. Falling prices reduce wages and business earnings, while debt burdens, contracted at fixed interest rates, remain unchanged. Unable to repay loans secured when prices were higher, the indebted attempt to raise cash by selling homes and other assets, driving down asset prices. Many are driven to default. Bankruptcies and foreclosures breed further unemployment, further defaults, and further drops in prices and incomes. During the Depression in the 1930s, prices fell nearly 20 percent, driving thousands of indebted farmers off the land and businesses into bankruptcy. In the past few years, falling prices have weakened the financial position of Japanese companies so severely that Japan's economy seems unable to recover. By 2001, inflation in the United States nearly ceased. The inflation rate in 2003 hovered just above zero, raising fears that prices and incomes will begin to fall—a potentially ruinous development in an economy where household debt levels have, for years, been rising faster than incomes.

To point out that inflation injures a mostly rich minority while deflation harms the indebted majority does not mean that inflation is desirable. Inflation redistributes wealth capriciously and dishonestly. It makes lending unprofitable and can disrupt the financial system. Moreover, inflation jeopardizes the finances of modestly situated households that, due to members' age or disability, must subsist on accumulated savings. Indeed, the more ordinary families rely upon past savings for retirement, health, and education needs, the more damaging inflation becomes. In an ideal world, inflation would be high enough to provide room for growth and pricing flexibility but stable enough that rentiers—including small-scale rentiers like retirees—could anticipate it and incorporate expected inflation into their financial plans.

The problem is that market economies, left to themselves, result in neither stable prices nor stable rates of inflation—any more than they exhibit stable rates of growth. Economic output rises and falls, as do price levels and inflation rates. Stabilizing prices, like stabilizing economic growth, requires economic policy—deliberate political intervention in the economy. The question is how the government should intervene. What precisely should governments do? How should they weigh the goals of price stability versus economic growth? Whose claims and concerns should take priority?

Since the end of the 1970s, policy makers in the United States and abroad have acted aggressively to control inflation. Preying on public anxieties about rising prices, elected officials in the United States empowered the Federal Reserve—a secretive, unelected, quasi-private body with intimate ties to the banking industry—to halt inflation. In Europe, anti-inflation policy was delegated to the minimally accountable European Central Bank (ECB). As we explain below, the methods central banks employ to avert price hikes turn out themselves to be so inequitable, so damaging to the real economy, and so corrosive to the democratic process that inflation, by comparison, looks positively wonderful. Moreover, in selling the public on the need to fight inflation, policy makers and media commentators have exhibited a remarkable indifference to the human costs of the inflation battle and a cynical willingness to exploit public ignorance of economics. The methods used to combat inflation may protect the savings accounts of ordinary families, but they do so by endangering the livelihoods of those same families.

SADO-MONETARISM

What causes inflation? Most readers probably learned in high school that inflation is a problem of "too much money chasing too few goods." As my own social studies teacher taught it, if the economy produces X goods and has X dollars floating about, prices will be stable. But if the government foolishly doubles the amount of currency in circulation, then $2X$ dollars will be chasing X goods, doubling prices of everything on average. This explanation was widely promulgated by the libertarian University of Chicago economist Milton Friedman in the 1970s and came to be known as the doctrine of monetarism. Why might the government do this? "From time immemorial," Friedman explained, "the major source of inflation has been the sovereign's attempt to acquire resources to wage war, to construct monuments or for other purposes."[7] The conservative economist F. A. Von Hayek concurred, arguing that "practically all governments of history have used their exclusive power to issue money in order to defraud and plunder the people."[8]

In Friedman's formulation, if federal authorities caused inflation by printing too much money, they could easily stop inflation by printing less. But monetarist doctrine rested on three flawed beliefs. First was the proposition that "money" could be clearly identified, tracked, and controlled by the government. Federal authorities do print currency and mint coins, but in a complex monetary economy, few transactions are settled with cash. Most of what circulates as money are liabilities created by the banking system—checking accounts, savings accounts, bank certificates of deposit, and so on. Banks create new deposit accounts every time they make a loan or issue a credit card and in doing so they expand the supply of money with no help from the government at all.

Second, monetarists presumed that the real and financial sectors of the economy operated in separate realms. They argued that the central bank could raise or lower the money supply with negligible long-term impact on the day-to-day operations of the job market or productive sector. Monetarists claimed that in the long run "money doesn't matter" and they meant this not in a moral or political sense, but in an operational sense.

Third, monetarists misrepresented (or misunderstood) the intricate political and economic processes that set off periods of inflation. They insisted that inflation was a "monetary phenomenon," a technical problem that could be corrected by technicians who would simply control the amount of money in circulation.

But inflation is not a monetary phenomenon. Inflation is the economic manifestation of a social conflict over the distribution of income and is intimately tied up with the state of a nation's labor relations.[9] Printing fewer dollars does not redress the conflict—rather, it shifts the balance of power in the economy to those with substantial financial wealth and weakens the ability of wage earners and borrowers to bargain successfully.

Periods of accelerating inflation are usually set off by what economics textbooks call "price shocks" and are sustained by "demand-pull" pressures. In the 1960s U.S. government outlays doubled as the private economy boomed, generating strong demand for workers and materials. The escalation of the Vietnam War contributed to tight labor markets; by the late 1960s unemployment rates averaged less than 4 percent, though many fast-growing industrial regions recorded rates of 3 percent or less.[10] To cope with shortages of workers, firms invested heavily in new technologies that boosted productivity. With unemployment rates low and over one-third of the workforce represented by labor unions, gains in output-per-hour were passed along to employees as higher wages. By the end of the 1960s productivity growth had slowed, yet American workers, protected by abundant jobs and strong unions, continued to demand and receive wage increases. These, employers passed along to consumers in the form of higher prices. Inflation, which had been a mild 1 to 2 percent, rose to 6 percent by 1970.

Then came the 1973 Yom Kippur War in the Middle East and the disruption of oil supplies. The price of crude oil—an input into everything from gasoline and pesticides to plastics and electricity—quadrupled in 1974.

In the context of strong unions, low unemployment, rising antiwar fervor, and social protest, soaring oil prices greatly exacerbated existing social discord. Oil sharpened the already tense conflict in Western countries over how income would be distributed between wages and profits. Would employees shoulder higher energy costs out of stagnant wages? Would businesses, facing higher costs but unable to raise prices correspondingly, suffer diminished profits? Could the cost be passed along elsewhere—to bankers in the form of lower interest payments or to foreigners in the form of higher export prices?

In some societies at some times questions of this sort can be broached directly in the political arena. Germany and

Sweden, for example, were as dependent as the United States on foreign oil, but got through the 1970s with minimal inflation. In national collective bargaining overseen by the government, labor and management representatives addressed the distributional consequences of higher oil prices directly and hammered out agreements over how costs would be allocated. The U.S. government had also used national economic policy to curb price pressures in the past. In both World War II and the Korean War, federal authorities imposed mandatory wage and price controls to prevent inflation and ensure that the costs of war were borne by all. When Vietnam War spending threatened to set off inflation early in the 1960s, the Kennedy and Johnson administrations convened annual labor-management conferences to set national wage and price "guideposts" and restrain inflationary pressures.

When continued war combined with rising oil prices in the 1970s, Keynesian economists advocated "wage-price controls" or "incomes policies" that would involve the government directly in negotiating the distribution of income. The Nobel Prize winner Robert Solow argued that inflation was probably "endemic to modern mixed capitalist economies that are determined not to tolerate severe slumps and that have the determination and the ability to avoid them." Since the disorder in the oil market would soon "burn itself out" in any case, national economic policies, judiciously applied, could target excessive wage or price hikes and minimize any damage caused by inflation.[11]

U.S. conservatives responded with alarm. As they saw it,

inflation amounted to a forcible confiscation of wealth, and incomes policies the culmination of the forced march to socialism that had begun with America's postwar embrace of Keynesianism. Keynesian policies, conservatives complained, first promoted endless government meddling in the market to promote "full employment." Next, unable to resist the wage demands of an empowered working class, the government planned to intrude in day-to-day business operations, dictating prices and disrupting the functioning of the market. Once wage and price controls began, warned the American Enterprise Institute economist William Fellner, "we shall be heading for comprehensively controlled societies, administered with reliance on significantly enlarged police power." Even if they did not lead directly to Soviet-style gulags, Fellner professed, controls would set the country on a slippery slope whose inevitable outcome would be "demoralization and low performance."[12]

The Nixon and Ford administrations called for voluntary wage and price restraints. Ford had millions of "Whip Inflation Now" buttons manufactured (but apparently never distributed) to enlist the nation in a patriotic anti-inflation crusade. But asking people voluntarily to stop defending their living standards—coming as they did from conservative administrations with weak ties to labor and unlikely to sanction noncompliant businesses—proved ineffectual. President Jimmy Carter promised in a 1978 speech that his administration "will not impose wage and price controls" and continued a policy of fruitless exhortation. Soon after Carter's speech, the Iran–Iraq conflagration doubled oil prices yet again.

As energy costs skyrocketed, growth slowed. Corporations, unions, unorganized workers, and smaller businesses each attempted, as best they were able, to pass costs along to someone else. In the absence of political institutions able to address economic tensions directly, distributional disputes inevitably spilled into the economic arena, with unions demanding wage hikes and businesses jacking up prices. The inflation rate rose inexorably.

In the end, everyone paid something. Wages fell through the late 1970s, though not dramatically. Corporate profits suffered. By 1973, Nixon detached the dollar from gold and let the exchange rate float on international markets. Over the next few years, the dollar dropped 20 percent on world markets. Oil-producing countries, imprudent enough to have priced their product in the fast-sinking U.S. dollar, ended the decade with less in their coffers than they may have hoped. But the financial world was hardest hit. For banks and their rentier clients, inflation was calamitous—it cut off their incomes, diminished their wealth, and, thanks to the falling dollar, weakened their standing in international markets.

Wall Street demanded relief. President Carter provided it in 1979 with the appointment of Paul Volcker as chair of the Federal Reserve. An avowed monetarist, Volcker attributed inflation to excessive growth in the supply of money. As chair of the Fed, the body responsible for monetary reserves to the banking system, he set about to curtail money growth and end inflation once and for all. But the flaws in monetarist doctrine revealed themselves almost immediately, with devastating consequences for the economy.

First of all, curbing money growth proved more complicated than it sounded. To stop the growth of money, the Fed must prevent banks from making loans. This the Fed accomplishes by driving up interest rates. Loans become so expensive that the only borrowers willing to borrow are those in such desperate straits that the banks are unwilling to lend to them. In 1980 the Fed Funds rate—the rate banks charge one another for short-term loans of cash reserves and which the Fed is able to control precisely—soared to 20 percent.

Second, high interest rates and restrictive credit conditions created economic chaos. Higher interest rates meant higher interest payments; income diverted to servicing loans translated into less spending on other things, less demand, less production, and less employment. Small businesses and other credit-dependent sectors like construction were battered as credit dried up or grew intolerably expensive. Unable to procure financing, they cut back output and laid off workers.

What Volcker accomplished then was not a reduction in the money supply—in fact, the Fed by the mid-1980s gave up any pretext that it could or was attempting to control the supply of money—but a seismic shift in the balance of U.S. economic power.

WHO IS THE FED?

ORIGINS OF THE FED

Congress passed the Federal Reserve Act in 1913. Legislation to create a U.S. central bank had been a key demand of the populist movement at the turn of the twentieth century. Adherents of this movement hoped that the bank would undermine the power of Wall Street "money trusts" and put an end to the periodic financial crashes, panics, and deflations that had plagued the American economy since the end of the Civil War. In the event of a financial panic, the Fed was to act as a disinterested "lender of last resort" to troubled banks—a role that had previously been played by self-interested private bankers like the House of Morgan. As President Wilson put it, the banks were to become "the instruments, not the masters" of the economy. The Fed was given unlimited ability to print currency or credit banks with fresh reserves (idle cash with which to make loans and repay depositors). However, from its very origins, the Fed was a conflicted institution, empowered with a public trust but answerable to the very banks it was supposed to supplant. During the bank panic of the 1930s, as anxious depositors clamored to reclaim savings that their banks had lost in the stock market crash, the Fed first sat on its hands and later made matters worse by *raising* interest rates. Searching through the Fed's archives, contemporary historians found that financial firms were lobbying the Fed intensely to raise rates and bolster their earnings.

STRUCTURE OF THE FED

The district banks The Fed consists of twelve Federal Reserve Banks, which are private entities owned by the member banks of their district. Member banks elect a board of directors, which in turn appoints a president of each district bank.

The board The U.S. president appoints a seven-member board of governors, based in Washington, D.C. Each governor serves for fourteen years; one of these is appointed to a four-year term as chair. The Fed chairmanship expires in the third year of a presidential election cycle. A one-term president will inherit the Fed chair from his predecessor and is unlikely to get to appoint more than two or three governors. Thus, neither the board nor the chair will usually be indebted to a sitting president.

The FOMC Policy decisions concerning interest rates fall to the Federal Open Market Committee, which meets every sixth Tuesday. The FOMC consists of all seven governors and all twelve district bank presidents. Decisions are generally made by consensus, but if there is no consensus, only five of the twelve bank presidents are permitted to vote. In between meetings, the Fed chair can convene emergency meetings or can act independently to raise or lower interest rates.

The FAC The directors of each district bank also select a representative to sit on the Federal Advisory Council, which meets behind closed doors with the board of governors at least four times a year. FAC members are usually officers of large financial institutions.

The Fed's structure makes it uniquely responsive to the voices of the finance industry. "It is fatuous," writes William Greider, "to pretend the Federal Reserve can somehow be insulated from politics. It is bombarded constantly with pleas and unsolicited advice from select interests. . . . Dialogues about monetary policy go on continuously between the Fed, financial markets, banks, brokerages and other major players both foreign and domestic. The only players left out of the conversation are the American people and, to a large extent, their elected representatives."

MONETARY POLICY

Although it possesses many tools to carry out its functions, the Fed has chosen to rely almost exclusively on open-market operations, the buying and selling of previously issued U.S. Treasury securities from and to the private financial market.

All member banks (all federally chartered and most state-chartered banks, representing about three-quarters of total bank assets in the United States, are members) must hold a certain percentage of their deposits as reserves—either as cash in their vaults or on deposit with their regional Federal Reserve Bank. When the economy grows, households and businesses spend more and borrow more. With each new loan they make, banks create new deposits and with each new deposit, the need for additional cash to hold in reserve. A bank that runs short of reserves can temporarily borrow extra funds from another bank that is holding more reserves than it needs. The market for bank reserves is called the Fed Funds market and the interest rate charged on these loans is the Fed Funds rate, or very-short-term (often referred to as "overnight") bank-lending rate.

When reserves begin to run out throughout the banking system, the Fed Funds rate will rise and, since this is a primary determinant of the banking system's cost structure, lending rates on business loans and mortgages will soon rise as well. To prevent interest rates from rising (or to drive them lower), the Fed will go into the open market and buy Treasury securities that are currently held by financial institutions or wealthy individuals. These securities represent money that the U.S. Treasury borrowed and has not yet repaid. To pay for the securities, the Fed credits the seller with new cash and the seller's bank with new cash reserves. Known as expansionary monetary policy, open-market purchases can also be thought of as liquidating the national government's debt. What was once a nonliquid (meaning that it could not be used to purchase goods) interest-bearing debt obligation of the

Treasury is converted to cash. (The Treasury must still pay interest on the debt, but now the interest goes to the Fed rather than to the public. The Fed keeps about $20 billion of this interest to finance its own operations and returns the rest to the Treasury at the end of each year.)

Conversely, if the Fed wishes to rein in bank lending and slow the economy, it will sell Treasury securities on the open market. When the Fed sells a security, the cash is debited from the buyer's bank account and hence from the bank's reserves. In this way, the Fed replaces liquid wealth with nonliquid assets and creates a cash shortage in the banking system. Scrambling for cash, the banks bid up the Fed Funds rate and other interest rates soon rise as well.

Quotes from President Wilson and William Greider are from the Financial Markets Center; its excellent primers on the Fed can be found at http://www.fmcenter.org.

Growth ground to a halt and unemployment reached nearly 10 percent by 1982—the highest level since the Depression. Real, inflation-adjusted interest rates rocketed to well over 10 percent in 1982 and remained at postwar highs until late in the 1990s. The calamitous economic impact of Volcker's assault on inflation probably cost Jimmy Carter the election in 1980.

In his eight years as Fed chair, Volcker also cultivated a reputation for arrogance and obfuscation in dealing with elected officials. The Humphrey-Hawkins Act of 1978 stipulates that Federal Reserve policy should promote "full employment, balanced growth and . . . reasonable price stability," and mandates that the Fed chairman testify before

Congress twice each year. Volcker's testimony was invariably cryptic, invoking obscure economic doctrine while disavowing any institutional responsibility for the economic downturn. Volcker insisted, for example, that the Fed's job was to maintain a stable supply of money. It did not control or even try to control interest rates and could not be blamed if interest rates soared to shocking levels. Critics pointed out that the so-called money supply seemed to gyrate wildly, despite the Fed's efforts. In response, Volcker grew evasive, declining to divulge first what its target was for money growth and later what definition of money the Fed was using. "The monetarist approach," William Greider points out in his 1987 account, was "politically valuable to [Volcker]. . . . As a political argument . . . it gave the chairman cover for the extraordinarily high interest rates he was imposing, a complicated rationale that most congressmen could not effectively challenge."[13]

Congressional liberals lambasted Volcker's opaqueness and disdain for democratic checks and balances, but Wall Street was ecstatic. Inflation rates fell and the real returns from lending soared. Furthermore, the Fed's new penchant for frequent meddling in the financial markets sent interest rates ricocheting madly. As interest rates move, so do the value of interest-bearing and interest-sensitive financial instruments like bonds, financial derivatives, and foreign currencies. Financial speculation—buying and selling assets to profit from changes in price—exploded. While the real economy stagnated, business on Wall Street boomed.

GREENSPAN AND THE MYTH OF THE NAIRU

In 1987 Reagan replaced Volcker with Alan Greenspan, a registered Republican, former adviser to the Ford administration, fervent libertarian, and disciple of Ayn Rand. Greenspan's Fed followed paths forged by Volcker. Under Greenspan, the Fed attempted to push inflation as close as possible to zero and keep it there. It fiddled incessantly with interest rates, generating constant volatility and profit opportunities for professional speculators. It evinced a willingness to raise interest rates even at the risk of higher unemployment and exhibited complete indifference to the plight of the unemployed. Greenspan fiercely guarded the Fed's political independence and, according to Bob Woodward's account, once threatened to raise rates simply to show the Reagan administration who was in control.[14]

By now, though, the Fed's claim that it did not control interest rates was no longer credible. The liberal economist James Galbraith decried the Fed's interest rate hikes as "taxation without representation." Democrats in Congress, especially House Banking Committee chair Henry Gonzales, assailed the Fed's secrecy and demanded that the Fed disclose its decisions and policy goals. After an embarrassing incident in which Greenspan was caught out in a lie concerning the Fed's record keeping, the Fed began to release a summary of its policy decisions, including its target for the Fed Funds rate.

Without monetarist doctrine to provide a rationale for

interest rate hikes, however, the Fed was vulnerable to political attack. To deflect criticism and justify Fed actions, Greenspan professed allegiance to a new economic doctrine known as the nonaccelerating-inflation rate of unemployment, or NAIRU. NAIRU theory went like this. Market economies have a "natural" rate of unemployment—representing workers who are ostensibly seeking jobs but who are, in fact, unwilling to take jobs at the prevailing market wage. This "natural" rate will vary from country to country; countries with extensive unemployment benefits and social insurance programs will have higher "natural" unemployment than countries with more "flexible" labor markets.

A national government, using fiscal and monetary policies, can try to stimulate job growth and reduce the unemployment rate below its natural level. But since the unemployed are unwilling to work at market wages, they will accept jobs only if wages rise and rising wages will then feed into rising prices. Result—inflation. With prices higher, the newly employed will demand even higher money wages to compensate, driving firms again to raise prices. Result—accelerating inflation that, NAIRU advocates claim, would spiral rapidly out of control.

NAIRU doctrine provided a definitive defense for restrictive monetary policy and unrelenting vigilance against inflation. Whereas monetarists denied that the Fed exerted control over interest rates, NAIRU proponents conceded that Fed policy impacted both interest rates and economic growth. However, the economy had a natural "speed limit," which the central bank could not override. If there was, as Keynesians maintained, a trade-off between job growth and price stability, then the Fed's statutory mandate to promote employment obliged it to err in favor of growth. But Greenspan's Fed maintained that no such trade-off existed when unemployment fell below the NAIRU. Elected officials might raise the speed limit—by ridding the economy of "disincentives" to taking jobs, like welfare, or to creating jobs, like corporate taxes—but that was another story, out of the Fed's hands.

Critics at liberal and labor-backed policy organizations like the Levy Institute, the Economic Policy Institute, and the Center for Full Employment and Price Stability immediately assailed the mythical nature of NAIRU. NAIRU advocates presented no data or studies of actual unemployed workers to corroborate their presumption that the jobless were unwilling to take available jobs. They provided no reliable estimates of what the "natural unemployment rate" might be. Proponents said 6 percent, but acknowledged that this rate might be "time varying," which is to say, impossible to determine. Galbraith complained that "the location of the natural rate can not actually be observed. Worse, the damn thing will not sit still. Not only is it invisible, it moves!"[15] Labor economists Jared Bernstein and Dean Baker pointed out that "there is no reliable way to figure out the NAIRU with enough certainty to guide policy makers," and even if there were, "there is no generally recognized explanation as to why, if we fall below the NAIRU, the inflation rate will continually accelerate."[16]

The NAIRU was thus an entirely theoretical proposition, a hypothetical construct that allowed the Federal Reserve to ignore its legal obligation to promote full employment. Greenspan himself was coy. Fed actions suggested that it believed the NAIRU to be 6 percent unemployment, but officially it declined to divulge a specific figure. Until late in the 1990s, though, Greenspan hiked interest rates each time the unemployment rate dipped much below 6 percent, launching what Fed press releases called "preemptive strikes" against possible "runaway inflation" and "overheating."

Six percent unemployment is a high rate of joblessness. It translates into some 9 million people without jobs and actively looking for work plus another 4 to 7 million who have either given up looking or have settled for part-time jobs because they could not find full-time positions. With such high levels of un- and underemployment it is hardly surprising that average wages fell through 1996. Economic Policy Institute director Jeff Faux complained that the Fed seemed to raise interest rates "every time an American worker is about to get a raise."

By the late 1990s, however, Greenspan began to revise his estimate of the NAIRU. Bob Woodward recounts the Fed chair's change of heart:

> The old belief held that with a low unemployment rate, workers would have the upper hand and demand higher wages. Yet the data showed that wages weren't rising that much. . . . Greenspan hypothesized at one point to colleagues within the Fed about the "traumatized worker"—someone who felt job insecurity in the changing

economy and so was accepting smaller wage increases. He had talked to business leaders who said that their workers were not agitating and were fearful that their skills might not be marketable if they were forced to change jobs.[17]

Operating on Greenspan's new theory of the traumatized worker, the Fed carefully eased off the brakes in the late 1990s, allowing the Fed Funds rate to dip below 5 percent in 1998. Unemployment fell below 4 percent with no sign of renewed inflation. Fed governor Janet Yellen, extolling the economy's performance, noted that, "while the labor market is tight, job insecurity also seems alive and well. Real wage aspirations appear modest and the bargaining power of workers is surprisingly low."[18]

Pundits hailed Greenspan as "the maestro"—the title of Woodward's fawning biography published in 2000—whose masterful orchestration of monetary policy created a "Goldilocks" economy, running neither too hot nor too cold, but just right. But the economy was not just right for the Fed. Wages began to rise briskly, most rapidly for those at the very bottom of the pay scale; the lowest-paid 20 percent of the workforce realized wage gains of 2 percent per year in the late 1990s and the U.S. poverty rate fell to 11 percent—a postwar low.

By 1999, Greenspan worried aloud that unemployment was becoming dangerously low. "Should labor markets continue to tighten," he warned in testimony to Congress, "significant increases in wages . . . will inevitably emerge," squeezing corporate profits and placing "our economic expansion at risk."

The immediate risk to economic expansion, it turned out, was the Fed itself. Although the inflation rate remained low—2.7 percent—the Fed moved aggressively to tighten credit conditions in 1999. Greenspan's Fed raised the Fed Funds rate six times over the next year. Its obvious intent was to curb growth in jobs and wages by provoking a recession.

By 2001, growth stalled and nearly 3 million U.S. jobs vanished. Now the Fed abruptly reversed course, slashing the key Fed Funds rate from 6 to 1 percent by 2003. Media commentators hailed the Fed for its bold and decisive response to the recession. Interest rates on home mortgages fell, setting off a wave of cash-out refinancings that sustained consumer spending even as jobs disappeared. But by late 2003, the economy was still sputtering. Inflation rates, running at only 2 to 3 percent during the boom, skirted perilously near zero. Thus *real* interest rates declined by far less than the Fed intended. For the first time since Paul Volcker's accession in 1979, restrained criticism of the Fed could be heard in the mainstream media.

Low interest rates fail to fuel business spending in an economic climate marked by depressed demand and underutilized capacity, analysts contended. The Fed's obsession with absolute price stability—zero inflation—left the economy vulnerable to deflation, which monetary policy is impotent to reverse (since nominal interest rates cannot fall below zero). Critics complained, in addition, of Greenspan's political duplicity—his willingness to lend his reputation to the defense of conservative tax cuts and weigh in on budgetary matters that are properly the domain of elected officials. The columnist Paul Krugman accused Greenspan of "providing political cover" to the Bush administration by waffling on the topic of the significance of federal budget deficits[19]—forcefully adhering to the crowding-out thesis against Democratic proposals to increase spending, but minimizing the issue when conservative plans to eliminate dividend or estate taxes were on the table.[20]

THE TRIUMPH OF CENTRAL BANKING

Whatever fault one may find with how the Fed made this decision or executed that policy, the problem with monetary policy lies much deeper. When Greenspan revised his estimate of the NAIRU in the late 1990s, he did so in the belief that productivity was increasing faster than government reports indicated. Thus, he reasoned, wages could rise without eating into profits, and the Fed, therefore, could keep interest rates low enough to accommodate continued borrowing and economic growth. Few commentators criticized or even remarked upon the fact that, in making such a determination, the Fed chair had taken upon himself responsibility for deciding the proper distribution of income between capital and labor.

Gradually, since the 1980s, central banks—insular, unelected, and unaccountable to the public—have been given the power to determine the appropriate distribution of national income between wages and profits. They have succeeded in this by depicting inflation not as a central issue of public policy, but as a purely technical process that can be controlled by neutral technicians with extensive training in the technical intricacies of finance. And so, with no real debate in any public forum, central bankers, with their extensive ties to the banking sector, have been ceded the right to answer for themselves the most momentous questions of national economic policy—what level of unemployment should a civilized society tolerate and who should suffer when war, or price shocks, or shortages, or economic distress create conflict over the distribution of income?

Before the 1980s, central banks rarely undertook significant policy moves independent of elected governments. In countries like the United States and Germany, central banks enjoyed statutory autonomy, but the political clout of progrowth labor groups and manufacturing interests restrained both the U.S. Fed and German Bundesbank from precipitate moves to curb growth. In France, England, and most other countries, the central bank fell under national government control, which addressed interest rates and inflation as part of a broader policy agenda.

By the late 1970s, however, manufacturing firms had grown weary of ceaseless labor unrest and wage disputes that imperiled profits. The traditionally progrowth goods-producing industries allied with the inflation-averse financial sector to support the transfer of policy-making authority from elected governments—always responsive to labor interests—to independent central banks, most responsive to the concerns of their prime constituency, the financial industry. In the United States, the result was Paul

Volcker's appointment to the Fed; in England, the election of combative monetarist Margaret Thatcher; in South America, the spinning off of monetary policy to unelected central banks and currency boards.[21] In continental Europe, anti-inflation political alliances culminated in the Maastricht treaty empowering the independent European Central Bank (ECB) to set monetary policy for all its signatory nations.

A fundamental tenet of postwar Keynesian economic policy was that central banks should be subordinate to elected governments. Monetary policy, Keynesians argued, is mostly useless in combating unemployment. Economic slumps follow booms precisely because, in the euphoria of the boom years, businesses invest too heavily in new facilities and equipment. Faced with ample capacity to produce, but too few sales to justify the capacity, businesses suddenly curtail orders for steel, glass, concrete, computer systems, broadband cable and DSL equipment, and all the other goods so intensely desired during the expansion. Once spending slows, lower interest rates do little to restore growth. Corporations saddled with underused and unprofitable office parks and factories are not likely to borrow and build more of the same just because credit is cheap. The sharper the downturn, the less impact monetary policy will have in stabilizing the economy. In a slump, Keynes wrote, lowering interest rates is akin to "pushing on a string."

Deficit-financed government spending—creating public jobs and incomes for the otherwise unemployed, generating a demand for the investment goods that private businesses no longer want—is the key to ending a slump.

Keynesians held that expansive, cheap money policy should be an adjunct to fiscal expansion, used to hold down interest charges on federal borrowing. A side-benefit of cheap money, Keynes said, would be the "euthanasia of rentiers"—the social demise of a class who derived its income from financial speculation and interest payments. The function of central banking should be to keep real returns on "near-monies"—short-term loans like bank deposits, Treasury bills, and commercial paper—close to zero. This would force lenders to commit their funds to long-term investment projects that enhance productivity and economic growth. Moreover, sustained low returns would eliminate trading gains for speculators who profited from constant fluctuations in interest rates and asset prices.

If low interest rates do little to end a slump, restrictive, tight money policies can effectively arrest economic growth. By raising interest rates in the midst of a boom, a determined monetary authority can dry up credit, send business spending into a tailspin, encourage short-term speculators, and counteract full-employment fiscal policies.[22]

The destructive power of monetary policy operates through four channels. First, simply by raising the cost of borrowing, high interest rates deter consumer and business spending. Large corporations are less affected, because most finance new investments from retained earnings. Smaller firms, though, borrow heavily to fund expansion, as do real estate developers and consumers planning to buy homes and autos. This spending slows when interest rates rise.

Second, to engineer a rise in interest rates, central banks create a cash shortage in the banking system. Lacking cash to meet their reserve needs, banks grow wary of writing loans—even loans carrying high interest rates—to any but their most credit-worthy customers. When monetary policy is restrictive, banks tighten lending standards and decline to roll over loans coming due, freezing out cash-strapped borrowers. This sort of "credit crunch" disproportionately impacts smaller firms, since large corporations generally enjoy higher credit-ratings and longer-established relationships with lenders.

Third, rising interest rates redistribute income from borrowers to lenders. Middle- and lower-income families typically own few interest-bearing assets but have considerable interest-bearing debt, so high interest charges promote an upward redistribution of income from indebted households to those with substantial financial wealth. According to the Fed's Survey of Consumer Finances, fewer than 10 percent of U.S. households hold any interest-earning bonds and only one in six owns a bank certificate of deposit (CD)—the only bank accounts that pay market rates of interest. The poorer 90 percent of U.S. households hold just 10 percent of bonds and 38 percent of bank deposits, but owe almost two-thirds of all personal debt.[23]

Finally, interest rates impact investor perceptions of what constitutes a reasonable rate of return. The overnight bank lending rate, which central banks control, establishes the market return on other short-term loans like U.S. Treasury bills. Very-short-term loans carry little risk for lenders. Since they will be repaid quickly, lenders will not be compelled to liquidate their positions at a loss, need not worry about inflation eating away returns over time, and the risk of default is minimal over short periods. Investment vehicles like stocks or bonds impose greater risks—of inflation, default, changes in asset values—and lenders demand correspondingly higher yields to compensate for increased risks. The risk-free return on Fed Funds sets a floor to financial returns. A Fed Funds rate of 20 percent (as in 1980) or 6 percent (as during most of the 1990s) is a high floor. To pay the higher lending rates and generate comparable returns on stock that financiers now demand, non-financial businesses need to pump up profits, or at least the appearance of profits, when short-term interest rates are high.

Monetary policy's impacts are largely negative. Central banks have difficulty reviving stagnant or depressed economies, but are adept at destabilizing robust economies. Moreover, the damage inflicted by tight money falls on the most economically vulnerable: families with heavy debts and cash-strapped small businesses and their heavily minority workforces. The economist Willem Thorbecke estimated that, after the Fed raises interest rates, "unemployment rises almost twice as much among blacks and Hispanics as among whites."[24]

Anti-inflation policies are intended to provoke recessions, suppress wage demands, and create unemployment. When the economy withstands central bank efforts to derail it—as the U.S. economy did for a time in the late 1990s—tight money promotes the financial volatility that feeds stock bubbles and exacerbates inequality. Restrictive monetary policies may not alone have triggered the outbursts of "irrational exuberance" and "infectious greed" bemoaned by Chairman Greenspan, but they laid the foundation for exactly the sort of finance-driven speculative growth that characterized the 1980s and 1990s.[25]

And to what end? Restrictive monetary tinkering was certainly successful in combating inflation—inflation rates in the developed economies have, for a number of years, been so close to zero that deflation is now a serious threat. Mainstream political and economic analysts rarely even mention the social costs of monetary restriction. This is unfortunate, for any reckoning of costs and benefits of our anti-inflation drive would almost surely conclude that the price has been, and continues to be, too high. At the minimum, such costs include:

Traumatized workers. Where inflation-control was handed over to independent central banks, the distributional conflicts that fed inflation were resolved through brute economic power. Soaring interest rates, rising unemployment, and sharpened social inequities left behind what Greenspan rightly called a "traumatized" workforce. Wage and salary earners, fearful for their jobs, abandoned any expectation that they could bargain, individually or collectively, for higher wages to cover rising costs. William Vickrey points out that central banks worry incessantly about a "wage-price spiral, [but] one never hears of a 'rent-price spiral' or an 'interest-price spiral.'"[26] This is because the entire point of restrictive monetary policies is to ensure that hikes in rent, interest, energy, housing, and health care costs will no longer be inflated away by empowered employees able to pass costs along. Higher costs will instead be borne by wage earners, and those with the least economic power—minorities, the uneducated, the unskilled—will suffer the greatest economic losses. Thus, *Fortune* magazine reported that, with health care costs expected to rise 24 percent in 2003, and wage increases barely "creeping along," employees will shoulder a disproportionate share of the burden—employee out-of-pocket health costs are expected to rise by 70 percent.[27]

Repressed growth. Despite spurts of speculative growth in the United States, Asia, and parts of South America during the 1990s, economic growth was lower and unemployment higher overall for the 1980s and 1990s than in prior years. The economists Gerald Epstein and Juliet Schor found that, throughout the world, countries with an independent central bank experienced less economic growth than countries that addressed inflation through national economic policy.[28] Andrew Glyn of Oxford University finds that high growth, low unemployment, and low inflation can all be achieved so long as a nation's political institutions are able to directly mediate distributional tensions.[29]

Impaired democracy. It is no accident that the moderate inflation of the 1960s and 1970s coincided with more egalitarian income distribution, stronger unions, and democratic ferment throughout the United States and Europe. The rise of central banking and anti-inflation policies severely weakens democratic institutions. Critical economic policy decisions are now in the hands of authorities who neither solicit public input nor engage in public debate, who in fact take pride in their opacity and bristle when elected officials presume to "interfere" with "their" decisions. Central bankers object to wording in their charters that compel them even to consider the social fallout of their policies.

In adopting the NAIRU doctrine, central banks have, since the 1980s, claimed for themselves the right to establish maximum allowable levels of employment, wage growth, and economic activity. Levy Institute president Dimitri Papadimitriou points out that the Maastricht treaty establishing the ECB "sets ceilings for inflation and government deficits and debt, but not for unemployment."[30] The Federal Reserve has lobbied Congress to alter the Fed's charter and relieve it of the obligation, under the Humphrey-Hawkins Act, to promote full employment, an obligation it routinely ignores in any case.

Proponents of independent central banks and zero-inflation policies argue that monetary policy is too important to be left to elected officials, who lack the "discipline" to "take away the punch bowl" when the economic "party" gets out of hand. Independent central banks can act as strict fathers, steering the economy with a firm hand to protect the value of wealth and ensure the smooth functioning of the financial system. A politicized central bank, in contrast, would imperil the profitability of financial firms, caving in to citizen suspicion of banks and sating public appetites for "class warfare."

But this argument is self-serving. Monetary policy itself is an instrument of class warfare, the repercussions of which independent central banks barely acknowledge. University of Massachusetts economist Robert Pollin points out that "by focusing on inflation as such rather than on the issues of income distribution and profitability," central banks have elevated the priorities of the wealthy to "the status of a nationally shared concern."[31] A democratically structured monetary authority would be forced to broaden its focus and address the social impacts of its policies forthrightly. In a public debate over inflation, questions of who gets what, who should bear the costs of price shocks, and how much unemployment is acceptable would be laid clearly on the table. If one looks at the diversity of experiences in Europe, Pollin notes, "one can see clearly that it is possible to create policies and institutions through which low unemployment and manageable inflation can be combined."[32] A wide-ranging public forum on inflation would examine the institutions and policies that have allowed countries like Ireland, Sweden, and the Netherlands to promote full employment without unleashing inflationary distributional battles.

In February 2003 the Bureau of Labor Statistics issued a report showing that prices had jumped unexpectedly in the previous month. It attributed the sudden surge in inflation in part to a sharp rise in energy prices, caused by the combination of severe cold in the Northeast and disarray in energy markets as war with Iraq loomed. Commenting on the report, David Wyss, the chief economist at Standard and Poor's, said, "The report shows that energy prices could still hurt us. The Fed doesn't have as much room to play with."[33] This sentiment reflects precisely the bind in which anti-inflation central banks have placed us.

With the Fed in control of economic policy, prominent economic commentators simply assume that oil-supply disruptions will be met not with public discussion of how to share the costs of war among the populace but with restrictive monetary policy. The Fed, it is taken for granted, will make certain that wage earners do not gain the economic power to pass the costs of war along.

CHAPTER FIVE

THE ALMIGHTY DOLLAR

When my daughter was in sixth grade, her class spent an afternoon learning about money. Children were shown pictures of ancient coins and cowry shells and invited to think of new or different things that might be used as money. The lesson plan was characteristically lightweight, the point apparently being that "money can be anything"—shells, beads, ears of corn, pieces of metal, or slips of paper. This American school lesson might have amused officials in Ecuador, who that very week had defaulted on their international debt for the lack of 45 million U.S. dollars—the only sort of money acceptable to Ecuador's creditors. Like most elementary school forays into economics, the sixth-grade lesson did not delve into the social nature of money or encourage speculation on the connections between money, wealth, and power. This is unfortunate, for if Ecuador could have paid its debt in brass coins or cowry shells, the world would be a very different place indeed.

What money is, what power it confers, what value it commands, and who issues it are fundamental political issues in any monetary economy. Nowhere are these questions more urgent and contested than in the contemporary global economic arena. Both the international financial debacles of recent years and the endlessly ongoing debt crises in Africa, Asia, and South America result from creditor efforts to control the perquisites of wealth in a rapidly globalizing economy.

FREEING CAPITAL

Money is, of necessity, a public good. National governments print it and enforce its use by mandating that the local currency be "legal tender" for discharging debts and paying taxes. So long as money is controlled by the state, there exists the potential that governments will redefine its value for political purposes, tolerating inflation and diminishing the value of accumulated wealth, using the state's power to borrow or print money to exert public control over resources or removing critical services altogether from the monetary economy.

The wealthy have thus sought to remove money-printing functions from those sectors of government most susceptible to popular pressure. Money printing cannot be privatized, but it can be quasi-privatized, relegated to autonomous and undemocratic central banks, like the Fed or the European Central Bank. In the global arena, however, there is no comparable entity to control money, and this is a perpetual source of concern for global businesses that may operate in dozens of individual states, each with its own individual currency.

A United States—based corporation producing toys in the

Philippines figures its earnings in dollars, but needs pesos to pay Philippine workers and purchase local supplies. Earnings of foreign subsidiaries of American firms generally accrue in the currency of the foreign country, yet shareholders want profits in dollars, so companies like Coca-Cola or Disney must sell their gourdes, pesos, dinars, and pounds to pay for imported materials and to return earnings to the United States. The same problem faces international banks and investment managers—shares on the Argentine stock exchange are purchased with pesos, but American investors want their gains sent home and distributed in dollars.

This converting back and forth of one currency for another is both costly and risky. National governments control the rules governing conversion—how much wealth can be taken from the country, what exchange rate will apply, even whether money can be converted at all—and national governments have been known to change the rules, entrapping foreign investors in the local economy who watch in despair as the currency's international exchange value plunges.

Until late in the 1980s, virtually every country in the world (the United States, Canada, and Switzerland were among a very few exceptions) restricted the movement of money across its borders. Called capital controls, these restrictions were thought essential to national sovereignty in economic affairs. Without capital controls, the wealthy can effectively thwart economic policy initiatives by mounting "capital strikes"—selling their local money for foreign currencies, devaluing the currency, and absconding with the nation's wealth. Most governments therefore imposed limits or waiting periods on capital movements, proscribed borrowing and lending in foreign currencies, and fixed the rates at which local money would exchange for foreign currencies.

Capital controls need not interfere with international trade, as long as the government allows importers and exporters to convert currency. But they seriously impede international investment. As multinational corporations (MNCs) expanded global operations throughout the 1980s and 1990s, they began pressuring governments to eliminate capital controls. An American company producing appliances in Italy for the European market did not want to be stuck holding its earnings forever as lira in Italian banks. International businesses wanted the freedom to trade lira for dollars or pesos for yen, and international banks, following their corporate customers across the globe, lobbied intensely to free capital movements, essential if they were to compete for business in foreign countries.

Acceding to pressure from corporate and financial interests, many European governments lifted capital restrictions by the end of the 1980s. Asian and South American governments, often at the prodding of the International Monetary Fund (IMF), followed suit in the 1990s. By the end of the 1990s, China was one of very few large economies to restrict cross-border capital movements, though a number of less-developed countries (LDCs) have recently reinstated controls.

If transferring monetary policy from normal avenues of

democratic accountability to central banks was critical to the rise of finance in the United States and Europe, lifting capital controls represented a decisive victory for financial interests internationally. Once governments opened the floodgates, money poured out, igniting explosive growth in international money trading, international borrowing and lending, and global investment of all sorts. By 2002, an average $1.5 to $2 trillion dollars changed hands each day on international currency exchanges, an annual rate amounting to ten times total world income and nearly fifty times total world trade.

As this sea of cash sloshes from shore to shore, it generates heavy surf for the rich industrialized countries. Exchange rates are now highly volatile and exporters in the rich G7 countries occasionally get battered when a soaring euro or plummeting yen prices them out of world markets.[1] For scores of poorer nations, however, the financial tides unleash tsunamis of debt, capital flight, currency collapse, poverty, and depression.

THE DOLLAR STANDARD

To understand the workings of the global financial system, it is useful to imagine oneself in the shoes of a person or corporation in an LDC who has acquired substantial financial wealth—a Saudi oil magnate, a Brazilian business owner, a British multinational, or a U.S. financial firm with global investments. Your wealth consists largely of financial assets that, when reckoned objectively, are little more than pieces of paper and computer entries the value of which fluctuates with market and political conditions. If some of your assets are held in Brazil, their value will vary with the Brazilian economy and stock exchange, with the Brazilian inflation rate and the exchange rate of the Brazilian currency—the real.

The question is to what degree you care about the external value of your Brazilian assets—what they are worth outside Brazil, in terms of a foreign currency. Clearly, non-Brazilians will care about this very much. So, increasingly, do Brazilians. As transportation, communications, immigration, and increased trade and investment integrate economies more closely, the wealthy see themselves more and more as denizens of a global, rather than purely national, economy and reckon their financial positions in global, rather than national, terms.

But what is the global financial standard? Until the 1930s, gold served this purpose. The wealthy distrusted national governments and the monies they issued and demanded that governments convert local currencies for gold at fixed rates of exchange. Rigid adherence to the gold standard was a condition for attracting not only foreign wealth but, since capital was free to come and go, for retaining domestic wealth. Neither governments nor private firms could hope to borrow from their own financial markets in their own currency and from their own residents unless the currency was seen as "sound"—that is, of stable value in terms of gold. Wealthy lenders shunned countries seen as "unstable," trading their currencies for gold or for that of another country deemed more reliable.

Today, the U.S. dollar serves as a global standard. To keep domestic wealth from fleeing the country or to attract foreign funds into the country, LDC governments face intense pressure to guarantee the dollar value of their local currencies. Only a few countries can evade this standard. Japan, Britain, Switzerland, and the combined euro economies, all rich nations with established networks of international banks and corporations, are able to borrow in their own currencies and face little pressure to insure investors against dollar losses. But financial interests spurn the currencies of LDCs and will hold assets denominated in these currencies only if assured that the dollar value of their wealth will remain secure.

Protecting the wealthy from inflation and from the threats to their wealth implied by public borrowing and pro-employment economic policy exacts an enormous toll on the economies of the United States and Europe—chronic joblessness, financial turmoil, heightened inequality, and impaired democracy. These quandaries facing the rich nations are largely of their own making—policies governments adopted under pressure from the finance industry and which they could, with sufficient political will, reverse. LDCs, however, face pressures not just from domestic elites but from abroad, especially from the IMF, which controls LDC access to global capital markets. Further, because investors demand protection of both the internal and external value of wealth held in poor countries, LDCs are trapped in a policy bind that is more draconian, more destabilizing, more contradictory and unpalatable than any rich nation would tolerate.

THE DEBT TRAP

When residents of Pakistan or Paraguay buy maize or medicine from the United States, they must pay with U.S. dollars. If they haven't earned enough dollars selling their own exports, they must borrow—from the IMF, the World Bank, a Western government agency, or a commercial lender. Foreign currency loans are problematic for poor countries. When Citigroup loans funds to an American business, it fully expects the business to realize a stream of earnings from which the loan can be repaid. When the IMF or World Bank makes foreign currency loans to poor countries—to finance deficits in their international payments and allow them to buy goods abroad—no such foreign currency revenue stream is generated, and the debt becomes a burdensome obligation that can be met only by abandoning internal development goals in favor of export promotion.

Few poor countries can balance their international accounts on a regular basis. Most need what the rich countries have to sell, yet offer little that the rich countries need to buy. Because poor countries often produce a limited range of primary commodities for export—coffee, paper pulp, lumber, cocoa, bauxite, rice—even the most tightly managed poor nation is only an earthquake or crop failure away from a foreign currency debt. The current free-trade milieu makes balancing one's international books more difficult, since countries are not free, under World Trade Organization rules, to impose new tariffs, duties, or other restrictions on imported goods. The United States may openly spurn global trade agreements—the Bush administration slapped new tariffs on steel imports to shore up Republican electoral support in 2002—but poorer, weaker countries must tread more carefully.

So over the years most LDCs have accumulated significant international debts. Of 156 countries classified by the World Bank as low- or middle-income countries, 147 are also classified as "indebted." Once a foreign debt is incurred, interest and other debt-servicing charges mount quickly. Because few countries manage to run trade surpluses large enough to pay interest regularly, service charges are rolled over into new loans and the debt balloons. This is why, despite extraordinary efforts by many indebted LDCs to pump up exports and cut imports, the outstanding foreign currency debt of developing countries has quadrupled since 1980.[2]

Until the 1970s, LDCs avoided foreign currency debts through a combination of trade restraints and capital controls—restricting imports either directly, through tariffs and trade barriers, or indirectly, by restricting residents from obtaining foreign exchange. But in the early 1970s, soaring oil prices pushed many countries into deficit and a number of South American governments took out sizable dollar loans from international banks. Banks were eager to lend. At the time, large global banks were awash in dollars deposited by the Organization of the Petroleum Exporting Countries (OPEC). They actively sought out borrowers in South America and the loans, guaranteed by governments with close ties to the United States and paying relatively high interest, were immensely profitable, at least initially. Bank lending officers pressed funds upon LDC governments for development projects, trade finance, business expansion. Some of the borrowed money was used to pay for oil, some for capital equipment to construct roads and dams, and some, raked off by corrupt government officials, found its way into numbered accounts in Switzerland or Panama.

The dilemmas intrinsic to foreign currency borrowing were apparent almost immediately. In 1974 Cheryl Payer published a book presciently titled *The Debt Trap*, warning that these loans were inherently unsustainable and would mire the borrowing countries in debt for years to come.[3] Large borrowers like Mexico and Brazil staggered under the debt load for a while, borrowing more each year to cover continued trade deficits and borrowing again to pay the interest on prior borrowing. Restrictive monetary policies in the United States (see chapter 4) sent interest rates soaring in the early 1980s, precipitating a crisis for the indebted countries. Mexico threatened default. The U.S. Treasury and the Fed hastily assembled a bailout promising new loans to Mexico with which to service the old loans.

Over the next decade, chastened commercial banks gradually withdrew from such international lending. The IMF stepped into the breach, arranging financing for LDC governments, restructuring private debts, and supervising repayment programs. None of this made a dent in the size of the debt, which continued to swell. By the end of the 1990s, 138 developing countries—virtually the entire developing world—had collective foreign currency debts of $2.5 trillion and were under IMF supervision. The indebted nations range from middle-income countries like Brazil, Ecuador, Argentina, and Mexico, with debts in the hundreds of billions, to dirt-poor nations like Mozambique, whose debt-servicing charges far exceed the country's annual export earnings.

The IMF response to the LDC debt crisis exemplifies the principles of finance-driven, "sound money" economics. The IMF draws its staff from mainstream economics doctoral programs and from the finance industry. Established in 1944, its voting and membership structure reflect the balance of economic power at the end of World War II. Just under half the votes (45 percent) are held by the G7 countries. The Netherlands and Switzerland, with 22 million residents between them, have more combined votes than China, home to 1.2 billion—more than one-fifth of the world's population. Saudi Arabia, the world's thirty-fourth largest economy, gets more than twice the votes of Brazil, the eighth largest. The United States, with 4.5 percent of the world's people, commands by far the largest voting share— at 17 percent it has three times the votes of the next largest vote-holders, Germany and Japan.

IMF headquarters is in Washington, D.C., a stone's throw from the U.S. Treasury, and even supporters acknowledge that the Treasury and IMF consult closely, so closely that critics claim the IMF is little more than the foreign-policy arm of the U.S. Treasury Department.[4]

Once ensnared in a debt trap, LDCs are cut off from most international credit until or unless they forge an agreement with the IMF. Known as structural adjustment or austerity programs, IMF agreements generally direct countries at a minimum to balance the national budget, stamp out inflation, and eliminate capital controls.

The first two requirements rule out Keynesian-style fiscal and monetary stimulus and set the country on a course of domestic austerity. The IMF prohibits full-employment policies in part to foster "flexible" labor markets. With public income supports and employment programs slashed, wages are free to plunge, making the country more attractive to multinational manufacturing firms and their investment dollars. But mostly, fiscal and monetary austerity guarantee that national economic policy will be mobilized to protect the power and privileges attaching to accumulated wealth and hence make the country more "attractive to investors."

In fact, though, the rationale for domestic austerity hardly matters. Once LDC governments consent, as a condition for debt restructuring, to the last requirement—free capital markets—the die is cast. The markets themselves will effectively veto any public policy perceived as threatening to financial interests. And to the IMF's demands, the financial markets will add a further stipulation—that the government stabilize its exchange rate against the dollar.

HOT MONEY

Eliminating capital controls, the former U.S. Treasury secretary Lawrence Summers once declared, opens up backward LDCs to "foreign financial service providers and all the competition, capital and expertise they bring with them."[5] For indebted countries, the potential benefits of open capital markets are compelling. Borrowing foreign currency saddles the government with an oppressive debt, ceaseless debt-servicing obligations, IMF intrusion, and foreign reprisal if the loan is not promptly serviced. Open capital markets, theoretically, allow governments to borrow in their own currency without incurring direct foreign-currency debts.

The United States, for example, has an international debt of gargantuan proportions. American residents import far more than they export—$500 billion more in 2003—and have amassed a foreign debt of over $2 trillion. But U.S. "debt" is composed of U.S. assets owned by foreigners—stocks, bonds, bank deposits, government securities, real estate and manufacturing facilities, loans to U.S.-based businesses and households—all denominated in dollars. The United States finances its international trade deficit by opening its capital markets to foreigners. If Americans send more dollars abroad than foreigners want to spend on American goods and services, foreigners can spend the balance buying U.S. assets instead. Such debt entails no foreign-currency servicing obligations for the U.S. government, no commitment to repay anything but dollars, and no IMF scrutiny of U.S. affairs.

The prospect of financing international obligations by selling assets denominated in their own currencies seemed an alluring alternative to debt for LDCs. With strong IMF encouragement, many embarked upon "financial liberalization" programs, opening their doors to Western financial interests, hoping to reel in dollars and euro and yen with the bait of high interest rates, friendly tax rules, and casino-style stock exchanges. Indebted governments also put public assets—water systems, oil, minerals, phone services, electricity, schools, hospitals, pension programs—on the auction block to lure investors.

But the global debt trap was not so easily eluded. Wary of becoming ensnared in global backwaters, international investors demanded that LDCs trolling for dollars promise a stable exchange rate against the dollar, so earnings could be converted and brought back home. These demands proved impossible to satisfy. If investors are free to come and go with their wealth, trading pesos or lira for dollars at will, then exchange rates, for all intents and purposes, will be set in the marketplace—the relative price of dollars and pesos shifting with each shift in supply and demand. Governments cannot promise stable exchange rates when their currencies are bought and sold freely on global financial markets. What they must instead do is promise to "defend" the exchange rate. They do this by accumulating reserves of foreign currency—building up stockpiles of dollars by running trade surpluses, privatizing public resources, or borrowing from international lending agencies—then, if the currency's value begins to drop, these reserves are expended in buying back the local currency, thereby propping up its price.

When this first-line defense fails—and it eventually does, because LDC reserves of foreign exchange are no match for the resources of the global financial markets—all fiscal and monetary tools must be mobilized in defense of the currency. The central bank hikes interest rates sky-high—to 50, 70, or 100 percent—to convince investors of the government's seriousness (we will strangle our economy to protect your profits!). The central government cuts spending and raises taxes, to convince financial markets that the state is prudent, conservative, and committed to the ideals of the financial industry. Once LDC officials allow investors to buy and sell the currency, the better to repatriate earnings or play the local stock exchange, they relinquish control over economic policy. Once capital is freed, financiers move in and dictate the terms on which they will stay.

The dilemmas of financial liberalization for LDCs should have been glaringly obvious. But under pressure from the IMF and G7—as well as from local entrepreneurs eager to cash in on the global economy—and amid cheerleading for the virtues of free markets by the media and international economists, LDC politicians ignored the contradictions. In the mid-1990s, with finance ascendant and fortunes being made, those who warned of hidden perils or looming crises were written off as Cassandras. Thomas Friedman's best-selling 1999 book, *The Lexus and the Olive*

Tree, urged forward-looking LDC politicians to don "the golden straitjacket" of fiscal and monetary austerity and follow "the electronic herd" to wealth and modernization.[6]

But the dangers soon became too plain to overlook. In the mid-1990s Western financial firms were bullish on Asia and on "emerging markets"—countries that had recently opened up their financial systems —generally. U.S. stocks, for the past few years, had recorded phenomenal returns and portfolio managers were looking to score equally impressive gains in international markets. They poured billions into stocks, bonds, banks, real estate, and business lending in East Asia, South America, and the former Soviet Union, expecting megareturns and a piece of the action as the former second and third worlds embraced global capitalism. In return, emerging market governments promised full and free convertibility of their currencies at fixed exchange rates against the dollar.

The author Barbara Garson, who followed her own bank deposit to Thailand in the mid-1990s, watched as American dollars financed an economic boom, buoyant job growth, and soaring incomes in Bangkok. "Rapid economic growth —8 percent growth," she writes, "translated directly into something you could see and feel on the streets of Bangkok. It's like musical chairs played with more chairs than people." By the middle of the year, however, investors began to worry that the fixed exchange rates couldn't hold. The funds pouring in to Thailand and other LDCs added up to considerably more than national treasuries could guarantee with their existing foreign exchange reserves. Worry turned to panic.

Foreign financial firms first pulled out of Thailand, selling baht for dollars and euros. As the baht's value collapsed, panic turned to rout. International financial operators were soon selling won, ringgit, and rupiah in an effort to cut potential dollar losses and get their funds safely back to Europe and the United States. In the ensuing capital flight, Asian stock prices plunged and the values of the Thai, Korean, and Indonesian currencies collapsed.

The governments of the affected countries attempted to hold the tide by lending their reserves of foreign currency to indebted businesses or buying back their currencies from speculators on financial exchanges. South Korea used up some $30 billion this way. This money soon ran out. Western banks refused to make new loans or roll over old debts. Asian businesses defaulted, cutting output and laying off workers. As the economic situation deteriorated, panic intensified. Asian currencies lost from 35 to 85 percent of their value, driving up import prices and pushing down the standard of living. Businesses large and small were driven to bankruptcy by the sudden drying up of credit; within a year millions of workers had lost jobs while the prices of basic foodstuffs soared. Suddenly, Garson explains, "they were playing musical chairs with many fewer chairs than people . . . substantial things, not just blips on a screen or entries in a ledger, but real stuff like food, clothing, friends and security disappeared."[7]

In 1998 the crisis spread to Russia and Brazil and by 1999 to Ecuador and Argentina.

THE REAL DEBACLE

In 1994 the Brazilian finance minister Fernando Cardoso introduced a new currency, the real. Lauded in international financial circles, the Real Plan was to serve two goals. First, Brazil's income distribution is among the world's most unequal and the country had long been torn by intense distributional battles that a weak political system was powerless to resolve. The consequence was high inflation and attempts by the wealthy to evade capital controls and trade their cruzeiros (the former currency) for dollars, depositing the proceeds in banks outside the country. Second, with nearly $200 billion in foreign loans, Brazil had the largest foreign debt in the world and the need to work with the IMF to raise dollars for debt service placed the government under constant strain.

Under the Real Plan, the government declared an end to the sporadic foreign-exchange controls of the past; the new real would be fully and freely convertible into other currencies and would be pegged one-to-one against the U.S. dollar. This would ensure financial investors against exchange-rate loss while protecting the wealth of the Brazilian elite, who, as is common among the upper crust in South America, figure their net worth increasingly in U.S. dollars. But just as important, the policy strictures entailed by a pegged exchange rate would finally curtail inflation. Because monetary and fiscal policies would be now marshaled in defense of the new real, they could no longer be used to mitigate domestic conflict.

The Real Plan, so it was said, would set off an economic boom in Brazil. Foreign investors would pour funds in and the local elite, notorious for moving money overseas, would keep their wealth in the Brazilian economy. For a time, the plan worked. The combination of full and free convertibility and a pegged exchange rate was a lure to foreign and domestic financial interests. Their confidence in the plan was evidenced by sizable inflows of cash from abroad, easing the heavy costs of servicing Brazil's foreign currency debt. But the economic contradictions of the peg were soon evident.

By 1998, financial players began to worry that the real was overvalued. Because price inflation in Brazil, though lower than in the past, was higher than in the United States, a fixed exchange rate distorted export prices and hurt Brazilian export industries.[8] Financiers worried legitimately that the government, in a pinch, would not or could not maintain the peg. Asian countries after all had also promised fixed exchange rates with the dollar, and look what had happened there.

Suddenly financiers began pulling funds out of Brazil, selling reals for dollars, plunging the Brazilian economy into a crisis from which it has not yet emerged. For a time, the government tried to stem the panic. Under the direction of Arminio Fraga, the former manager of a Wall Street hedge-fund, Brazil raised short-term interest rates to 50 percent, announced cuts in federal pensions to "restore investor confidence" in the real, spent billions in foreign currency reserves to support the exchange rate, and sought dollar loans from the United States and IMF with which to purchase real on global markets and protect the all-important dollar peg.

Officials from the IMF and U.S. Treasury Department urged Brazil on, advising the government to raise interest rates and cut government outlays. Defense of the real became a condition for releasing additional IMF monies, though the economy was clearly staggering. Not until Brazil had spent half its foreign-exchange reserves defending the peg did U.S. officials, afraid that Brazil would be unable to make scheduled payments on its external debt, reluctantly advise the government to give it up and let the currency float. But by then the damage was done. Economic growth had sputtered to a halt; unemployment rose, and with it, poverty—in a country already notorious for shocking levels of deprivation. The Brazilian economy, in short, was sacrificed for the sake of the real.

The real debacle helped propel Worker's Party candidate Luis Inacio Lula Da Silva to victory in Brazil's 2002 presidential election. Campaigning against IMF-sponsored sound-money policies, Da Silva promised to cut interest rates, protect public pensions, raise civil service wages, and implement ambitious new social welfare initiatives including a Zero Hunger plan. By early 2003, however, Lula had raised interest rates twice, ordered billions in public spending cuts, and endorsed a "reform" package promising more fiscal retrenchment. As the Brazilian political scientist David Fleischer explained to the *New York Times*, politicians like Lula "have no choice if [they] want favorable treatment from the markets."[9] And a country owing over

$200 billion to foreign creditors needs the good favor of the markets.

Within a few months of taking office, Lula's popularity ratings had sunk below 50 percent as leaders of his own party accused him of "putting bankers ahead of people."

THE CONVERTIBILITY CATASTROPHE

A few years before Brazil introduced the real, Argentina announced its own sound-money plan. Like Brazil, Argentina had a crushing foreign debt, perpetual problems with capital flight, highly unequal income distribution, and chronic inflation. The Argentine convertibility plan promised to end inflation, entice foreign investment dollars, and persuade Argentina's wealthy to keep their funds at home. Masterminded by the Harvard-trained finance minister Domingo Cavallo, the plan eliminated Argentina's extensive capital controls and made the peso fully convertible at an exchange rate of one peso per dollar. As a further inducement to foreign investors, the government embarked on an extensive course of privatization, selling off state-owned wineries, oil refiners, steel mills, military manufacturers, banks, airports, railways, highways, postal, gas, electricity, and telecommunications services. The public pension system was largely dismantled and replaced with private investment accounts.

The new exchange rate was to be guaranteed by a currency board, a central bank dedicated solely to confining growth in Argentina's money supply to growth in its dollar reserves. Promising not to issue domestic currency except in proportion to foreign exchange reserves sounds straight-forward, but in fact, it is not a simple promise to keep. As discussed in chapter 4, banks, not governments, create most of what circulates as money. Constraining monetary growth, in practice, means implementing a set of intensely restric-tive economic policies, intended to forestall wage demands, curb bank lending, restrain public spending, and demon-strate to financial markets that the government is firmly committed to the peg.

Initially the convertibility plan seemed an unqualified success. Nearly $20 billion flowed in from abroad as multi-national firms snatched up Argentina's public resources—90 percent of government assets were sold. Wealthy Argentines repatriated money held overseas and global fi-nancial firms booked loans and purchased bonds issued by Argentine businesses. But most were denominated in dol-lars. The currency board instilled such confidence that foreign banks were certain Argentines could meet their liabilities by trading pesos for dollars at the promised rate. Altogether, some $40 billion poured into Argentina be-tween 1992 and 1997. The IMF proudly pointed to Argentina as a model of what could go right when a nation embraced monetary and fiscal discipline.

But problems with the convertibility plan were evident from the start. The country bought a temporary reprieve from debt-repayment headaches, but only by accumulating greater debt. Argentina's external debt more than doubled during the 1990s. Inflation was tamed by the government's extremely austere policies, but unemployment, which averaged 6 percent in the decade before the convertibility plan, rose to an average 12.8 percent from 1992 to 1998. When the Asian "flu" spread to neighboring Brazil in 1998, tumbling the real, currency traders began selling pesos as well, guessing that Argentina would cave in. The peso held, but its strength relative to the real made Argentine goods expensive in Brazil, Argentina's largest trading partner, and the Argentine economy began to collapse. Speculators now bet heavily against the peso, daring the government to stake its dollar reserves on the peg.

In the end, the economy crashed as the wealthy pulled funds out of local banks and sent the dollars abroad. Only after months of crisis and civic disorder, including the resignations of three presidents, did a fourth president, Ferdinand Duhalde, disband the currency board, impose capital controls, devalue the peso, and freeze dollar-denominated bank accounts. By the time Duhalde took action, the official unemployment rate stood at 20 percent, though more broadly defined estimates suggested that as many as four in ten workers were unable to find jobs. By 2003, half of the county's population earned less than the government's official poverty line of 140 pesos per year.

In 2002 Argentina announced that it was unable to make a scheduled $4 billion payment on its foreign debt. As of this writing, it has repeatedly threatened default and has been unable to reach an agreement with the IMF.

BAILOUTS

The contradictions involved in promising currencies that are both convertible and stable should be obvious to international financial institutions like the IMF. Rich countries would never make such guarantees, nor do financial investors expect compensation when the dollar or yen or euro drops 20 or 30 or 50 percent. Dollars and yen and euros are international currencies, the forms in which the wealthy and powerful measure their wealth and power. They are thus truly money, while the real and peso and baht are mere bits of paper. International investors prefer not to hold them without assurances.

LDC efforts to insure international investors are pointless in the face of burgeoning speculation in currency markets which now turn over $1.5 trillion to $2 trillion dollars each day. The gains to be won by attacking LDC exchange rates—high interest rates and massive foreign exchange reserves committed to the currency's defense—are irresistible to speculators and lead inevitably to the crises that afflicted Thailand, Argentina, Brazil, and many others. The policy of defending exchange rates with a combination of high interest rates and foreign exchange reserves has been a virtual invitation to professional speculators. Just as finance professionals lured American workers into the financial markets with 401(k)s, then promptly separated them from their savings, the industry pressured LDCs to "liberalize" their markets, then—in 1998 alone—captured $130 billion in LDC savings, as governments threw away hard-earned reserves buying up their currencies on global exchanges, futilely attempting to "defend" their currencies.

But this is just the beginning of the losses suffered by LDCs at the hands of the financial markets. As the LDC financial crises unfolded, IMF officials jetted from capital to capital to arrange "bailouts," agreeing ultimately to lend some $150 billion to the various afflicted nations. When announcing these loans, the press used terms like "emergency assistance" or "international rescue package," leading the casual reader to presume that the money will be spent on food for the hungry or aid for the jobless. In fact, bailout funds are meant to "help" countries make whole any losses to international banks and brokerage houses. The "assistance" was then added to the outstanding foreign debt of affected LDCs.

In the late 1990s Western financial firms began lobbying for even more reliable protection against potential losses in emerging markets. The U.S. and U.K. Treasury Departments proposed establishing a $90 billion fund of public money to avert currency crises. Under this plan, G7 governments and the IMF would underwrite the finance industry's speculative ventures into emerging markets before, rather than after, they turned sour. In this way when financiers withdraw their funds from a country and send the currency into a tailspin, they can collect on their losses from the fund immediately, without the tedious and time-consuming delays generated by negotiations over IMF bailout packages.

The industry has also been working overtime to squelch defensive LDC reactions. During the Asian crisis, the gov-

ernment of Malaysia chose to reimpose capital controls
to protect the ringgit. Then–Treasury secretary Lawrence
Summers decried the action as a "catastrophe." Despite repeated crises and heavy criticism, the IMF has apparently
intensified pressure on indebted countries to liberalize
financial markets. In fact, in the midst of the Asian crisis,
the IMF held a conference to consider whether "it was time
to add an amendment to the IMF's Articles of Agreement to
make liberalization of capital movements one of the purposes of the Fund."[10]

In 2002 Anne Krueger, deputy managing director of the
IMF, advanced a plan for a "sovereign debt restructuring
mechanism"—a kind of international bankruptcy process
by which crisis-stricken nations like Brazil and Argentina
could seek legal protection from creditor demands. The
plan was opposed by the Bush administration and by Wall
Street groups, which, according to the *Washington Post*, "re-
acted with outrage to the idea, warning that capital flows
to emerging markets would dry up if creditor rights were
infringed."[11]

Critics of IMF and U.S. policy have, of course, noted that
the combination of free-flowing capital and bailout funds
are a boon to banks and other creditors. Such IMF critics as
former World Bank economist Joseph Stiglitz and Columbia
University's Jeffrey Sachs complain that the global financial
markets menace world economic stability. But the financial
crises are not mistakes, nor are the devastated economies of
Asia unfortunate side-effects of IMF policy errors. They are
the inevitable and predictable result of a flawed system.

South America's and Asia's bankrupt businesses, insolvent banks, and jobless multitudes have become the spoils of what the Canadian economist Michel Chossudovsky aptly calls "financial warfare."[12] The gains to be won from these financial hit-and-runs are immense.

First, there are the bargains to be had once the target country's currency has collapsed and its firms are strapped for cash. Years of effort, for example, by the Korean elite to keep businesses firmly under control of state-supported conglomerates called *chaebols* were undone in a matter of months by the Asian crisis. In the midst of the crisis, Citigroup, Goldman Sachs, and other firms were snatching up ownership of Asian banks and industries. With currencies down 15 to 60 percent and stock prices down 40 to 60 percent, Asia became a bargain-hunter's paradise. Nor are assets the only bargains. In the wake of the economic collapse in the LDCs, prices of basic commodities fell steadily. By the late 1990s, copper, tin, lumber, paper pulp, cocoa, coffee, and rice were dirt cheap for consumers in the United States and Europe.

Second, there is the higher tribute that countries, once in debt peonage to global banks, must pay on both old and new loans. Since the crisis, LDCs are perceived as more risky environments in which to do business. To compensate for greater risk, international lenders doubled or tripled the interest rates that they charged on foreign currency loans to emerging markets.

Next, there are the people themselves, impoverished and committed by their governments to an endless course of domestic austerity and debt repayment. Before the financial crisis of the late 1990s, the affected Asian nations—unlike the countries of South America and Africa—owed very little to the rest of the world. Many nations, like Korea, had run sizable trade surpluses for years and accumulated impressive hoards of foreign exchange. By opening their capital markets to G7 lenders, allowing domestic firms to borrow on global markets, and promising to maintain a fixed exchange rate against the dollar, they spent down their reserves and ended up instead with a massive sovereign debt. The financial and economic crises in Asia and South America added millions to the numbers of people engulfed in poverty and unemployment.

Finally, there are the governments themselves, the ultimate prizes to be won. It is no accident that conditions imposed by the IMF on cash-strapped governments entailed a major loss of national sovereignty. Debt agreements are hammered out in lengthy secret meetings between affected governments and high-ranking IMF officers. Dictators and elected politicians alike endure public humiliation, as the IMF imposes loan conditions that strip countries of sovereignty, dismantle public employment, welfare, and pension systems, or force dramatic transformations in the target countries' legal and political systems.

In response to such criticism, IMF officials were quick to point out that the usurped governments often were not themselves paragons of democracy and virtue. But this is beside the point. The motives of the IMF and its G7 sponsors are themselves an intolerable affront to the democratic process. In his 2002 book, *Globalization and Its Discontents*, Joseph Stiglitz complained that IMF agreements and bailout terms were shrouded in such secrecy that details often were not known even to World Bank officials in a joint mission, much less to the citizens of the affected countries.[13]

Stiglitz recalls that the IMF, as originally envisioned after World War II, was intended to promote global employment and macroeconomic stability by acting as a lender of first resort to sovereign states with international payments problems. Today, effectively controlled by G7 countries and dominated by finance ministers and central bankers, the IMF purports to look after the stability of the global economy as a whole, but in fact pursues the narrow interests of the global financial elite.

GLOBAL DEFLATION

The current system of global finance functions as an almost perfect mechanism for transferring wealth from the world's poor to the rich. Control over resources, labor, and markets—once seized and held by force of arms in colonial wars—is now won through the device of currency crisis, foreign debt, and IMF austerity plans.

Before the debt crisis engulfed the developing world in the late 1970s, most poor countries—even those with corrupt and autocratic governments—saw "import substitution" and internal development as the foundation of their economic futures. Countries in Africa, Asia, and South America hoped to build domestic manufacturing capacity by promoting local firms, boosting consumer purchasing power, and developing markets for locally produced industrial goods.

But foreign debts have forced virtually all poorer countries to renounce internal development goals. Instead of promoting real investment in local industries by local businesses, countries vie for injections of foreign investment dollars to be used for debt service. Indebted governments offer up their "comparative advantage" in exploitable labor, cheap resources, and lax safety standards to transnational corporations who receive, in return, control over wealth, resources, and people.

The logic of debt repayment requires that both human and natural resources be exploited rather than conserved. Indebted governments must promote short-term foreign-exchange earners like timber and beef, rather than nurture the long-term growth of local pharmaceutical or consumer goods industries. Environmental protection and labor rights suddenly become "luxury goods"—too costly because they might drive away transnational investors like Disney or Chiquita. Entire nations are turned into export platforms, where human labor and natural resources are transformed into the foreign exchange needed to service nearly $2.5 trillion in accumulated LDC debts.

Austerity in the LDCs exacts a toll on the rich economies as well. The competition for investment dollars places the desperately poor residents of developing countries in direct competition for jobs with G7 workers. Cornell labor specialist Kate Bronfenbrenner found that, whether American corporations actually move jobs overseas or not, they routinely wield the threat of moving to counter union-organizing drives and extract contract concessions.[14] Advocates of labor and environmental protections worry that the financial plight of LDCs fuels a "race-to-the-bottom" by which mobile corporations pit countries against one another in the bid for dollars, weakening social welfare, labor, and public health standards throughout the world. The fear that unrestrained competition among LDCs will undermine the hard-won regulations on business practices in the G7 countries—child labor proscriptions, minimum-wage guarantees, limits on weekly working hours, workplace safety regulations, worker compensation programs, employer contributions to public pension programs, laws regulating the use and disposal of hazardous materials—have sparked worldwide protests.

LDC austerity exerts another serious though less noted impact on the world economy—the pull of global deflation and depression. Policies that enhance a country's appeal to financiers and enable it to make timely payments on foreign debt also contribute to curtailed demand for products around the globe. When Brazil or Ecuador or Indonesia lay off public employees, raise interest rates, and curb import spending, then America and Germany and Japan encounter stagnant world markets for their computers, autos, and video cameras. If the countries of the developing world must export more and import less, those in rich countries will import more and export less.

This is not to suggest that expanded international trade

is a zero-sum game, that one nation's success always entails another's failure. Expanded trade and export promotion *can* engender virtuous cycles. In the best-case scenario, Brazil's exports increase the incomes that allow Brazilians to purchase American goods; the United States' heightened sales generate income from which Americans purchase additional Brazilian goods, and so on, to the mutual benefit of workers and consumers everywhere. But international trade stimulates self-reinforcing economic growth only in the context of a financial structure that offers countries reasonable options for managing capital flows, exchange rates, and payments deficits.[15] An international financial system geared primarily to protect the value of monetary wealth and insulate financiers from risk and loss is a fetter on global growth.

In the current system, governments need to protect themselves from the financial fallout of international trade, avoiding imports, husbanding foreign-exchange reserves, and curbing internal growth to avert disastrous capital flight. Between 1996 and 2002 developing countries nearly doubled their holding of foreign currency reserves to over $1 trillion—idle funds held in public treasuries used to service debt and protect currencies from attack by speculators. This is in addition to the $136 billion in reserves that LDCs lost to speculators in the late 1990s.

These reserves are accumulated at great cost to the working populations of the LDCs, who labor hard to produce goods destined to be consumed by foreigners. But they impose a cost as well on U.S. and European workers, whose jobs grow less secure as export markets shrink. Just as savings can disrupt the flow of income and slow growth in a domestic economy, the hoarding of international cash reserves reduces demand and slows global economic growth. In the domestic economy, the distortions caused by savers can be offset by expansionary monetary and fiscal policies that promote spending and keep income and goods flowing freely. Not only do no parallel mechanisms for counteracting global savings exist in the international economy, the current international system actually rewards those nations that successfully accumulate reserves.

This is not a hypothetical problem. History provides ample lessons in the destructive potential of a global economy built upon a privatized, finance-driven payments system.

Until the 1930s, industrialized market economies participated in the gold standard. During World War I, the gold standard was briefly suspended, but it was restored by 1925. Under the rules of the gold standard countries agreed to maintain fixed exchange rates, convert their currencies into gold upon demand, and allow full and free international exchange of the currency. As a practical matter, these rules obliged participating nations to maintain sizable reserves of gold, so that they could buy back any surplus currency that found its way into the international banking system as a result either of capital flight or a trade deficit. Maintaining the gold standard also necessitated that countries prevent inflation at all costs, since a general rise in prices would price exports out of world markets and place pressure on the government to devalue.

In the event of a payments deficit, national governments routinely raised interest rates to attract currency to the local financial markets and slowed their economies to reduce spending on imported goods. In addition, they depleted reserves to prevent depreciation and, if reserves ran out, borrowed from international banks to defend the currency. The gold standard, in other words, required austere economic policies of deficit countries. Deficit countries had to try immediately to close a deficit in their external accounts and they did this mostly by raising interest rates. If they did not follow the rules, they risked capital flight and being cut off from international credit.

Under the gold standard, countries depressed and deflated their economies rather than devalue their currencies. Governments tried to run trade surpluses and hoard the resulting gold inflows, so as to maintain high levels of gold reserves. As a result, nations with successful export industries did not share their success with others by using the export income to purchase imports. As the economic historian Peter Temin has written, adjustment to payment imbalances was "asymmetric"—countries paid a high penalty for running out of gold, but none for accumulating gold.[16] Since rapid growth in incomes is often accompanied by growth in spending on imported goods, growth itself became dangerous. Central banks stood ready to slow the economy at the first sign that external payments were going into deficit.

Governments responded to unemployment with efforts to cut wages rather than create jobs, generating intense social and class conflict.

In the event of a general economic downturn, as occurred in the 1920s and 1930s across Europe and the United States, countries were quick to impose tariffs and "export" their economic problems to their neighbors, exacerbating political tensions. Since a refusal to abide by the gold standard rules left a country without access to international credit, closing the economy entirely to trade was often the only viable political option when a country faced payments problems. The dissolution of the gold standard and lack of any alternative global financial agreements probably contributed to the Great Depression, culminating in World War II.

At the close of World War II, officials from forty-four nations, led by the United States and Britain, met in Bretton Woods, New Hampshire, to construct a set of rules intended to remove economic policy from the hands of international bankers and place it under the control of governments. The Bretton Woods Agreement established the IMF and World Bank, the brainchild of British economist John Maynard Keynes and U.S. Treasury official Harry Dexter White. Many would be surprised today to learn that the IMF, as Keynes had originally conceived it, was designed to be a lender of first resort to countries needing foreign currencies to purchase goods abroad. Had it developed as Keynes intended, the IMF would have stripped financiers of the power to dictate policy as a condition for credit. The IMF would also, as Keynes and White conceived it, eliminate the deflationary biases of the gold standard. Whether an individual country could borrow abroad to finance expansionary policies would no longer be decided by bankers, but by governments sensitive to political and strategic considerations.

As it turned out, the United States generously provided billions in direct aid to Europe after World War II under the Marshall Plan, so the IMF's money-lending facilities were barely needed for the reconstruction of Europe. By the 1970s, the largest of the G7 economies enjoyed enough stature in global markets to finance payments imbalances with their own currencies—they could take it for granted, that is, that any excess pounds or yen sent abroad in payment for goods would return as payment for British or Japanese assets. Smaller European economies like Italy and France bound themselves together in a European Monetary System (precursor to the euro), enabling them to gain preferential access to international markets as well. By the mid-1990s, the IMF's sole remaining function was to act as a global bill collector for the LDCs.

Today, two international financial orders coexist in the world. For the G7 and other euro-countries, international financing is relatively unproblematic. Deficits are financed with capital inflows. If investors fail to purchase enough assets to use up the surplus currency sent abroad, traders will sell the excess dollars or euro and the exchange value of the currency will depreciate. For large, diversified, and self-sufficient economies, depreciation carries little sting. A devalued currency makes imports more expensive, but countries like Japan and the United States can produce most of what they need domestically, so dearer imports bolster the sales of domestic firms.

The LDCs, on the other hand, inhabit a world very like that of the discarded gold standard. Because financial markets demand open borders, low inflation, and a stable currency, the poorer countries face all the contortions and restrictions of a gold standard, foreclosing almost any reasonable options for domestic policy. But the gold standard countries of the early 1900s had a final escape route—albeit one fraught with geopolitical perils—closing off their borders and focusing on internal development. This route is closed to the LDCs. IMF programs almost always insist that indebted countries practice "free trade."

These two international financial systems foster two separate and unequal economic systems. The rich countries, having superior access to finance, are rendered more stable, and their stability makes them magnets for the world's financial wealth. The poor countries, unable to procure stable access to finance, are rendered unstable, and their instability repels investors. Success breeds success and failure generates failure.

The costs of these arrangements are high, for residents of rich and poor countries alike. In the absence of international political agreements to resolve payment issues and negotiate responsibility for debt and adjustment more equitably, the U.S. dollar has become the de facto global currency and private banks the de facto arbiters of global economic policy. The dollar's global role makes it highly valued in comparison with other currencies and allows the

United States to finance huge payments deficits at virtually no cost. For Americans this translates into cheap, plentiful imports—a boon for consumers but a disaster for unskilled American workers, whose job prospects have deteriorated steadily over the past two decades as manufacturing jobs moved abroad. Enforced stagnation in the LDC economies translates into hundreds of millions of unemployed or underemployed and an estimated 2 billion people living on less than two dollars per day.

In the early 1990s a series of speculative attacks on the currencies of smaller European countries convinced governments that they could not hope to navigate the international financial waters unless they banded together to create a unified currency. The introduction of the euro in 2002 has been a blessing for European corporations doing business abroad and has given European consumers preferential access to cheap imports from the LDCs. But in creating the euro, European citizens ceded control of macroeconomic policy to the deeply conservative European Central Bank (ECB) in Frankfurt. Europeans now lack even the basic fiscal tools for combating recessions. Unemployment rates in the largest European economies have been ranging from 8 to 11 percent since 2002.

In an integrated and open world economic system, economic events in one economy spill across borders. Addressing unemployment, poverty, and inequality requires not only that national governments recognize their mutual interdependence but that they coordinate their policies in ways that promote growth, stability, and an equitable distribution of the world's wealth. Over the past two decades, however, as governments surrendered their policy tools to the global financial industry, the world has become more dangerous, the world economy more volatile.

The solution to global economic disorder is not hard to imagine. Above all, LDCs should be permitted to pay for needed foreign goods and services in their own currencies, rather than scrambling endlessly for the foreign currency that they do not print, do not control, and cannot dependably earn in sufficient amounts through exporting. Private investors shun LDC assets, but the governments of the world could agree to hold LDC currencies even if the markets will not. The world needs an international payments arbitrator, democratically structured and publicly controlled that would allow countries to settle payments imbalances politically, as all matters that bear on the well-being of humanity should be resolved politically.

A global settlements institution would benefit poor and rich countries alike, since the advanced nations could export far more to developing countries if those countries were able to settle accounts on more advantageous terms. But such an institution would dramatically shift the balance of power in the world economy. If LDCs were not so desperate for dollars, international corporations would find them less eager to sell their resources and citizens for a fistful of greenbacks. That nations rich in people and resources, like Brazil and South Africa, can be deemed bankrupt for lack of foreign exchange is an unacceptable artifact of a global finance system designed to enrich the already rich.

CHAPTER SIX

A BETTER DEAL

With the demise of the postwar Keynesian consensus, a new economic orthodoxy has slowly taken root. This doctrine today suffuses political discourse in the United States, permeates the institutions of the European Union (EU), and is pressed upon the less-developed nations by IMF missionaries. Its major tenets go like this:

- Governments should balance their budgets.
- Central banks should combat inflation.
- Taxes on capital—that is, on accumulated wealth and very high incomes—should be negligible or nonexistent, so as to reward thrift, encourage saving, and promote investment.
- Expensive public commitments like universal pensions, health, child welfare, and education programs discourage thrift and encumber investors with heavy taxes. They should be curbed or cut.
- Citizens should instead save for major life events like aging and raising a family.
- Governments should promote personal thrift and financial planning by exempting savings from taxation, while

taxing consumption more heavily—for example, by raising sales and excise taxes while cutting taxes on capital
incomes. In this way, ordinary households will be
encouraged to build financial wealth and reap the
rewards available to investors.

· With taxes cut, government spending tamed, and each
responsible for his own welfare, the private economy will
thrive and the need for interventionist economic policy
wane.

· In the unlikely event that the economy sputters,
stabilization policy should be handled by the central
bank, which can, assuming inflation is not a problem,
lower short-term interest rates enough to entice spend-
ers to take on more debt and encourage economic
growth.

· Money should be free to move across borders. When it
is, investors will reward responsible governments with
investment dollars and discipline irresponsible governments with capital flight.

Called "supply-side" economics by its adherents and
"market fundamentalism" or "neoliberalism" by its critics,
the thrust of this new economic doctrine is that governments bear no responsibility for the overall levels of output
and employment in their countries, nor for the real welfare of their citizens. These are to be left to the marketplace.
To the extent that a government must sometimes expend resources on things other than defense, promotion of trade,
and protection of property, its activities should not be al-

lowed to imperil the interests of the financial sector—should not be financed by borrowing or taxing wealth, should not entail restrictions on capital mobility, and should not ignite even mild inflationary pressures.

Those whose incomes derive from work rather than ownership, according to the new orthodoxy, are best served not by government but by hard work, thrift, self-reliance, and an unfettered marketplace. The possibility that a market economy may fail to provide equitable access to jobs and resources is simply dismissed by supply-side advocates. "Market failures" arise from government meddling in the economy, not from the economy itself.

Although the rhetoric of supply-side economics is ubiquitous, the full supply-side program is far from being realized. Its implications—draconian cuts in public spending, the introduction of regressive taxes, public inaction in the face of unemployment—arouse too much voter opposition. In the United States, where the now-dominant Republican Party professes unabashed allegiance to supply-side views, opposition to deficits was tabled in 2002–2003 in the hopes of stabilizing employment before the 2004 election.

Many European governments, facing rising unemployment, stagnant growth, and deflation, are in open rebellion against the EU Stability and Growth Pact. Both the French and German governments flouted EU limits on public-sector deficits; national officials snipe openly at the European Central Bank (ECB) and its inflation-averse chair, Jean-Claude Trichet, blaming the bank's obdurate refusal to cut interest rates for their weak and sputtering economies. Once-supportive Swedish voters recently rejected a referendum to adopt the euro and join the ECB. Voters throughout Europe spurn attempts to balance national budgets by cutting pensions, health, and other social benefits.

Resistance to the new financial orthodoxy also erupts periodically in the indebted countries. Argentina's newly elected president, Nestor Kirchner, promised to repudiate the country's "illegitimate" debt, renationalize the rail system, and build 3 million units of public housing. The Latin American Council of Churches urged indebted countries to embark on a campaign of "economic disobedience" against the "dictates of the international financial institutions"—defaulting on foreign debts, combating poverty, and providing jobs through massive public works.[1]

Despite these sparks of rebellion and resistance, though, the language and thrust of economic policy, in the United States and around the world, still faithfully reflects the interests of the wealthy.

Consider recent tax initiatives of the Bush administration. In 2003, the administration proposed abolishing all taxes on stock dividends, reducing the top marginal tax rate from 38.6 to 35 percent and allowing families to place up to $60,000 each year in tax-exempt savings accounts. Congress instead passed a bill cutting the top tax rate to 35 percent and capping the rate paid on both dividends and capital gains at 15 percent. Most stockholders hold shares in tax-sheltered retirement accounts already and so would not benefit from lower taxes on investment earnings; few Americans are in a position to save $60,000 per year; and a bare 0.7 percent of households earn enough to be taxed at the top rate. Citizens for Tax Justice estimated that two-thirds of the dividend cut alone would accrue to the richest 10 percent of households. A *Wall Street Journal* study concluded that the top three officers of Fortune 100 companies would receive an average $393,000 tax cut under Bush's plan. Sanford Weill, the embattled CEO of Citigroup, would save $7 million in taxes each year just from the abolition of dividend taxes.

When combined with cuts passed in 2001—which had already reduced the top tax rate and repealed federal taxes on large estates—the 2003 package, says the economist Thomas Piketty, will "rebuild a class of rentiers in the U.S., whereby a small group of wealthy but untalented children controls vast segments of the U.S. economy and penniless, talented children simply can't compete. . . . There is a decent probability that the U.S. will look like Old Europe prior to 1914 in a couple of generations."[2]

As debate proceeded in Congress and in the U.S. media, many commented on the inequities in the plan, but virtually nobody questioned the argument that breaks for wealthy investors benefit the economy and serve the general good. *Business Week*, a generally fair and reasonable magazine, asked readers to vote on whether strong growth spurred by Bush's tax cuts was worth the price of greater social inequality.[3] Democrats inveighed against the unfairness of the cuts and assailed them as budget-busters, but stopped short of attacking the basic premise that what's good for the financial elite is good for the economy.

Elected officials in Europe exhibit similar reticence in critiquing the assumptions of the supply-side doctrine. While balking at the strictures of the ECB, officials stop short of proposing alternatives to it. It has become impolitic to suggest that the interests of the wealthy are not those of the public at large, that protecting financial wealth may impose heavy costs on the economy. Political leaders in developing countries delight in pillorying the IMF, but offer few ideas for how to organize global economic policy differently.

Once politicians accede to the basic premises of supply-side economics and don the "golden straitjacket"—committing to unrestricted financial flows, to resist inflation at all costs, to balance the public budget, to create an environment friendly to "investors"—the die is cast. Policy is driven by the need to oblige the wealthy and protect their wealth or risk capital flight.

Keynesian and social democratic policies were founded on very different goals—creating jobs, promoting human development, and enhancing social welfare. Those policies doubled living standards in much of the world and fueled, in the industrialized countries, the growth of a large and economically secure middle-class. Today, liberals and progressives bemoan the victories of the right, yet lack a language and conceptual framework to challenge its premises. "Third-way" liberals, for example, advocate such devices

as "individual development accounts" and "microloans"—
by which governments would contribute to "personal wealth
accounts," giving everyone a stake in the financial economy.[4]

These and similar ideas remain mired in the myths of
finance. When one equates increases in financial wealth
with improvements in real well-being, then one can substi-
tute a collective commitment to social welfare with the quest
to create millions of little pots of gold.

REAL WELL-BEING

In the postwar period, the industrialized countries developed programs to prevent mass unemployment, promote
social welfare, and mitigate the impact of economic downturns. They were founded on the premise that real wealth
lies in the real economy—workers, facilities, productive resources, infrastructure—and well-being can be assured only
when individuals are assured a secure claim on the economy's output.

These programs increased the size and scope of government economic activities and public sector employment
and redistributed income through social welfare spending
and progressive taxes. With more income flowing through
the hands of ordinary households and the government, it
was hoped that economies would be less prone to downturns
caused by volatile business spending. Ordinary households
would have less need to save up against adversity, since social welfare programs protected them against expensive and
unpredictable events like ill health, a prolonged retirement,

and unemployment. Lower savings, in turn, would ensure that firms found buyers for the goods they produced.

It is commonplace to disparage such programs as "big government" intrusions that burden individuals with onerous taxes. Such aversion to collective provision makes sense in a world suffused with financial illusions. The macroeconomic interdependencies of a complex monetary economy—by which one person's spending is another's income and one person's job loss, another's falling sales—are largely invisible to individuals going about their daily life. Even when macroeconomic imperatives assert themselves through recessions and financial crashes, the language of economic policy discourages the public from envisioning the connections between their own and others' well-being.

Yet the case for a robust public sector is at least as much an economic as a moral one. Ordinary individuals and households fare better when they are assured some secure political claim on the economy's output, because secure claims on the economy render the economy itself more stable.

Dependable public claims, for one thing, create reliable income streams and employment. Universal public schooling, for example, requires that a sizable portion of national income is devoted to building, equipping, staffing, and maintaining schools. If backed by firm legal commitments to public education, such spending is less susceptible than private sector spending to business cycles, price fluctuations, and job losses.

Unfortunately, in the current U.S. economy, public schools raise virtually their entire budgets from state and local taxes, which oscillate with private sector spending, making education spending vulnerable to economic downturns. In 2003, as state and local tax receipts plunged, American public schools shortened the school year, slashed bus services, laid off janitors, and closed after-school programs to balance their budgets.

Efforts to raise municipal taxes and protect school budgets encountered strong voter opposition—understandable in a weak economy. Yet voters may find themselves worse off altogether as unemployed teachers, janitors, and bus drivers bid down wages and curtail their own spending. Public school retrenchment is driven not by a lack of schools, facilities, willing workers, or eager pupils, but from a lack of money. This lack could easily be repaired with federal funds, but that would entail higher deficits, ruled out by the discourse of finance.

A country that promotes economic security with dependable public claims on economic output can also obviate the need for individuals to amass sizable private savings. Social Security and other public pension programs, for example, provide the elderly with direct claims on the real economy in their retirement. Americans still need to save up for old age—Social Security benefits replace, on average, only one-third of prior earnings—but thanks to Social Security they can get by with less savings than they would need otherwise. Social Security reduces people's exposure to volatile financial markets and improves their average prospects for a decent retirement, but by reducing personal savings, it also improves the chances that income earned will translate into income spent, making the overall economy more reliable. Programs like Social Security align private behaviors and motivations with the public interest in a high level of economic activity.

In a weak economy, individuals coping with insecure job prospects are encouraged to balk at increased social spending. Yet programs that provide direct public claims on output substantially ameliorate the sting of joblessness and minimize the macroeconomic fallout of unemployment. Public schools, colleges, parks, libraries, hospitals, and health and disability insurance ensure that the unemployed continue to consume at least some minimal level of goods and services. Some may complain that social services give the jobless something for nothing, but the alternative for those with jobs can be considerably worse. Without social supports, the unemployed would be forced to withdraw altogether from the economy, pulling children out of schools, forgoing health care, dragging prices and wages down with them, and setting off destabilizing deflations.

THE REVOLT OF THE ELITES

During the last two decades of the twentieth century, as the rich grew richer, their interest in policies that provide universal claims on social output waned. The very-well-off do not need Social Security or public colleges—their high incomes allow them to purchase expensive services privately.

They resent paying taxes to support programs that they do not need and that, in any case, diminish the social status accruing to wealth.

Ordinary households, too, were discouraged from asserting direct claims on the economy and encouraged, instead, to emulate the rich and amass personal wealth. This was accomplished in part by the shifts in discourse and policy, documented in previous chapters, which reduced expectations that policy would be conducted on behalf of the broad public. But middle- and low-income households in the United States also confront actual and threatened retrenchment in programs that provide the public with direct access to economic goods and services.

Colleges and universities, for example, that were once "public" institutions now bill themselves merely as "publicly supported"—state subsidies now account for less than half their revenue, and this share is due to fall further as state and local governments retrench in reaction to the intense fiscal pressures of recent years. Publicly funded grants and loan subsidies have remained flat as tuition charges at both private and public colleges soared. Public housing funds were slashed in the 1980s and 1990s and replaced with "vouchers" to subsidize individual rent payments on the private market, though increases in market rents far outstripped the value of vouchers. Funding for maintenance of public beaches, parks, and recreation facilities has declined, driving vacationers away from public facilities. The Bush administration along with the Republican-controlled House of Representatives has floated pro-

posals to replace Social Security with private savings accounts, to convert Medicare from a publicly managed insurance system to a system of vouchers with which retirees can
purchase private insurance, to eliminate the federal entitlement to Medicaid and replace it with fixed grants to state
governments. In its 2003 budget, the Bush administration
floated the idea of replacing unemployment insurance with
a system of Personal Re-Employment Accounts, which
would provide unemployed workers with a fixed sum of
money ($3,000) in lieu of the current guarantee of six
months of benefits, presumably as an incentive for the jobless to find jobs.

These losses of social safety nets and shared resources
create anxiety about one's livelihood and future that need to
be recouped with greater private resources. As individuals
strive to amass private wealth, the rich, poor, and middle
class alike resist taxation or, indeed, any government policy that renders wealth less valuable or more difficult to
accumulate.

In a series of articles on the first Bush tax cut in 2001, the
New York Times profiled Dr. Robert Cline, an Austin, Texas,
surgeon whose $300,000 annual income still left him wor-
ried about financing college educations for his six children.
Dr. Cline himself attended the University of Texas, at a cost
of $250 per semester ($650 for medical school), but figured
that "his own children's education will likely cost tens of
thousands of dollars each."[5] Dr. Cline supported the 2001 tax
cut, though that cut contributed to an environment in which
institutions like the University of Texas raise tuitions, re-

strict enrollments, and drive Dr. Cline and others to seek private education for their children.

Unlike Dr. Cline, however, most people will never accumulate sufficient hoards of wealth to afford expensive high-quality services like college education or to indemnify themselves against the myriad risks of old age, poor health, and unemployment. When middle-income households do manage to stockpile savings, they have no control over the rate at which their assets can be converted to cash or the prices at which cash can be converted to real goods and services.

Virtually all people—certainly the 93 percent of U.S. households who earn less than $150,000—would fare better collectively than they could individually. Programs that provide direct access to important goods and services—publicly financed education, recreation, health care, and pensions—reduce the inequities that follow inevitably from an entirely individualized economy. The vast majority of people are better off with the high probability of a secure job and standard of living than with the low-probability prospect that they will win the lottery, beat the stock market, or best GDP growth.

A BETTER DEAL

It has become de rigueur in books on economic and social policy to close with a shopping list of the author's own policy proposals. I will demure from detailed policy proposals.

Good social policy is not formulated by academics hammering away in isolation at their keyboards. It evolves from honest and informed deliberation, respectful negotiation, and shared ethical values. Bad policy arises from dishonest rhetoric, cynical misrepresentation, bad-faith negotiation, and conflicting value systems.

The world today is in the grip of bad policy—bad not because the policies' impact, intent, or implementation are deficient, though this is often the case, but because the milieu in which policy is formulated is saturated with dishonesty, cynicism, and bad faith.

The purpose of this book is to contribute to an environment in which economic policy can be discussed intelligently and honestly. Since the 1980s, conservatives have waged a sustained battle to roll back the public sector, but their campaign has been waged largely through indirection. The ostensible goals are to balance the budget, encourage thrift, promote investment, and prevent inflation. The real objectives are to curb social welfare, eliminate progressive taxes, promote the financial interests of the wealthy, and curtail any remaining expectation among voters that the government may be a source of jobs, incomes, stability, or security. Since these objectives cannot be openly advocated, they are pursued obliquely. Macroeconomic rhetoric has become the battering ram with which broader social and economic objectives are won.

In this environment, it is impossible to know what kind of government or economy voters support, since the ques-

tion is rarely posed. So I will close this book not with a proposal but with a hope.

I would hope for a moratorium on faulty and misleading
economic rhetoric followed by an open and far-reaching
public discussion of the goals of economic policy and the
values that underlie them. Forget, for a moment, budget
deficits, the value of the currency, the inflation rate, the need
to raise stock prices or placate capital markets or repay debt
or save for the future. If these monetary issues were off the
table, if the citizens of the world were free to think and discuss policy without artificial barriers obstructing the discussion, what would they say? What would they want? What
values would they share?

In 2003, with Republicans firmly in control of the
House, Senate, and executive branch, conservatives grew
surprisingly forthright in stating their own ideologies and
underlying values. In a speech promoting the Bush 2003 tax
package, for example, Vice President Cheney told the U.S.
Chamber of Commerce, "Our administration's pro-growth
initiatives were the products of a very clear economic philosophy. The president and I understand that the government does not create wealth and it does not create jobs, but
government policies can and should create the environment
in which firms and entrepreneurs will take risks, innovate,
invest and hire more people."[6]

Milton Friedman, guru of right-wing economics and an
ardent foe of deficit spending, explained his support for the
2003 tax cuts and resulting deficits in a *Wall Street Journal*
editorial. "Deficits," he writes, "are probably the only effec-

tive restraint on the spending propensities of the executive branch and the legislature."[7]

"Unless there is gridlock from divided government," he later told the *New York Times*, "Congress will spend as much as the tax system. . . . Cutting taxes is the only way to restrain spending."[8]

Republican strategist Grover Norquist told the journalist Robert Dreyfuss that his goal was "to cut government in half in twenty-five years, to get it down to the size where we can drown it in the bathtub."[9]

So here, stripped of confounding rhetoric, is the philosophy of the right. Only private wealth is true wealth. Efforts to create public wealth are to be fought with tax cuts and deficits until the government—source of dams, irrigation systems, trains, buses, sidewalks, roads, highways, fire departments, trash collection, police protection, pensions for the aged, nursing home care, medical insurance, health research, colleges, after-school enrichment programs, playgrounds, parks, libraries, and beaches—is hopelessly gridlocked and can be drowned in a bathtub.

In a similar spirit of candor and forthrightness, let me close with my own economic philosophy. I believe that wealth is created by human beings, working together with the earth's resources toward shared goals, through private businesses, nonprofit institutions, cooperative ventures, and governments at all levels. I believe that markets, left to themselves, are unstable and generate needless inequity, insecurity, and joblessness, but that these flaws can be addressed through careful and flexibly designed public policy.

There are numerous models of successful public policy aligned with the private sector to create stable, secure, and sustainable economic systems. The range of particulars is probably quite wide, and an open, honest, and democratic society can experiment, learn from the experience of others, and discover which set of policies works for them.

NOTES

CHAPTER ONE

1. Thomas Piketty and Emmanuel Saez, "Income Inequality in the United States, 1913–1998," Working Paper no. 8467 (Cambridge, Mass.: National Bureau of Economic Research, September 2001).
2. Kevin Phillips, *Wealth and Democracy: A Political History of the American Rich* (New York: Broadway Books, 2002).
3. See, for example, Barry Bluestone and Bennett Harrison, *The Deindustrialization of America: Plant Closings, Community Abandonment, and the Dismantling of Basic Industry* (New York: Basic Books, 1982).
4. Robert H. Frank and Philip J. Cook, *The Winner-Take-All Society: How More and More Americans Compete for Ever Fewer and Bigger Prizes, Encouraging Economic Waste, Income Inequality, and an Impoverished Cultural Life* (New York: Free Press, 1995).
5. President's Commission to Strengthen Social Security, *Strengthening Social Security and Creating Personal Wealth for All Americans: Report of the President's Commission* (Washington, D.C.: President's Commission to Strengthen Social Security, December 2001).
6. Mark Maier, "Teaching about Stocks for Fun and Propaganda," *Dollars and Sense*, March/April 2001.
7. Lisa Singhania, "More Blacks Are Turning to Stocks to Secure Future," *Boston Sunday Globe*, July 8, 2000.

CHAPTER TWO

1. Robert J. Shiller, *Irrational Exuberance* (Princeton, N.J.: Princeton University Press, 2000).

2. Dean Baker and Marc Weisbrot, *Social Security: The Phony Crisis* (Chicago: University of Chicago Press, 2001). See especially chapter 5.

3. Thomas Frank, *One Market, Under God: Extreme Capitalism, Market Populism, and the End of Economic Democracy* (New York: Doubleday, 2000).

4. Quoted in Frank, *One Market, Under God*, p. 93

5. Federal Reserve Board, *Survey of Consumer Finances*, www.federalreserve.gov, 1998, and *Survey of Consumer Finances*, 1983–1989 Panel Survey.

6. Kevin Phillips, "Dynasties!" *Nation*, July 8, 2002.

7. Cited in Lawrence Mishel, Jared Bernstein, and John Schmitt, *The State of Working America, 2000–2001* (Ithaca, N.Y.: Cornell University Press, 2001).

8. Edward Wolff, "Recent Trends in Wealth Ownership," Working Paper no. 300 (New York: Levy Economics Institute, April 2000).

9. Alex Berenson, "Investors Hold On as the Market Heads Downhill," *New York Times*, July 21, 2002.

10. Connie Bruck, *Predators' Ball: The Inside Story of Drexel Burnham and the Rise of the Junk Bond Raiders* (New York: Penguin Books, 1989); James B. Stewart, *Den of Thieves* (New York: Simon and Schuster, 1991).

11. Edward Faltermayer, "The Deal Decade: The Verdict on the 1980s," *Fortune*, August 26, 1991.

12. David Wessel, "Why the Bad Guys of the Boardroom Emerged en Masse," *Wall Street Journal*, June 20, 2002.

13. William Greider, "Is This America's Top Corporate Crime Fighter?" *Nation*, August 5–12, 2002.

14. See Matthew Josephson, *The Robber Barons: The Great American Capitalists, 1861–1901* (New York: Harvest Books, 1962).

15. Stephen Achelis, Technical Analysis from A to Z, http://www.equis.com/free/taaz/oddlotbalind.htmlweb.

16. In their best-selling books, the Beardstown Ladies claimed to have averaged a 23.4 percent return on their investments. They subsequently admitted that returns had been only 9.1 percent—far below the average rise in the S&P for the period.

17. Gretchen Morgenson, "A Star Analyst Exits Loudly; Others Hide Backstage," *New York Times*, August 18, 2002.

18. Olga Kharif, "Telecom Analysts: So Many Bad Calls," *Business Week*, July 10, 2002.

19. "How Corrupt Is Wall Street?" *Business Week*, May 13, 2002.

20. Charles Gasparino, "Latest Fuel in Analyst Probe: Bonus Memos," *Wall Street Journal*, May 30, 2002.

21. "How Corrupt Is Wall Street?"

22. Jeff Faux, "Securing Pensions," *American Prospect*, March 25, 2002.

23. An investigation by the National Association of Security Dealers accuses Salomon Smith Barney of "spinning" shares in initial public offerings (IPOs)—giving shares at the opening price to favored corporate executives, who then sell the shares once the price jumps—in return for banking business. See Charles Gasparino, "Salomon's Grubman Resigns; NASD Finds 'Spinning' at Firm," *Wall Street Journal*, August 16, 2002. The House Financial Services Committee found that Bernard Ebbers, CEO of World-Com, pocketed $11 million from such deals over a four-year period. In some cases, the IPO shares allotted to Ebbers represented two-thirds of the total shares available to retail customers. See Suzanne Craig, "Offerings Were Easy Money for Ebbers," *Wall Street Journal*, September 3, 2002.

24. Faux, "Securing Pensions."

25. James Ridgeway, "Hijacking the Future: How Wall Street Is Taking Over Worker's Pensions," *Dollars and Sense*, September/October 1999.

26. Jeffrey Seglin, "Do Options Buy Silence?" *New York Times*, February 17, 2002.

27. Consolidated Complaint filed against Enron, cited in William Greider, "The Enron Nine," *Nation*, May 13, 2002.

28. Dennis Berman, "Before Telecom Industry Sank, Insiders Sold Billions in Stock," *Wall Street Journal*, August 12, 2002.

29. An investigation by *Wall Street Journal* reporters Marc Maremont and Laurie Cohen estimates that Mr. Kozlowski took another $135 million from Tyco in the form of forgiven loans and real estate purchases (August 7, 2002).

30. Mark Gimein, "You Bought, They Sold," *Fortune*, September 2, 2002.

31. *Business Week*, "Executive Pay Scoreboard," April 19, 1999; April 17, 2000; April 16, 2001; April 15, 2002.

32. Frank Rich, "State of the Enron," *New York Times*, February 2, 2002.

33. Alex Berenson and Lowell Bergman, "Under Cheney Halliburton Altered Policy on Accounting," *New York Times*, May 22, 2002.

34. Paul Krugman, "Everyone Is Outraged," *New York Times*, July 2, 2002.

35. Robert Brenner, *The Boom and the Bubble: The U.S. in the World Economy* (London and New York: Verso, 2002), p. 148.

36. Cited in Richard Oppel, "The Danger in a One-Basket Nest Egg Prompts a Call to Limit Stock," *New York Times*, December, 19, 2001.

37. Ellen Schultz and Theo Francis, "Business Lobby Guts Legislation to Curb Employer Stock in 401(k)s," *Wall Street Journal*, July 23, 2002.

38. Cited in Ellen Schultz and Theo Francis, "Companies Hot Tax Break: 401(k)s," *Wall Street Journal*, July 31, 2002.

39. Ibid.

40. David Leonhardt and Geraldine Fabrikant, "Many Chiefs Are Retaining Extra Benefits in Retirement," *New York Times*, September 11, 2002.

41. David Leonhardt, "Executive Pay: A Special Report; Perks Make Life Comfortable, Even in Retirement," *New York Times*, April 7, 2002.

42. Richard Oppel, "Companies Cash in on New Pension Plan; But Older Workers Can Face Penalties," *New York Times*, August 9, 2001.

43. Michelle Conlin, "Workers, Beware of Brave New Health Plans," *Business Week*, September 9, 2002.

44. Cited in Louis Uchitelle, "The Rich Are Different: They Know When to Leave," *New York Times*, February 20, 2002.

45. Jeremy Siegel and Peter Bernstein, *Stocks for the Long Run: The Definitive Guide to Financial Market Returns and Long-Term Investment Strategies*, 2d ed. (New York: McGraw-Hill, 1998).

46. Dow Jones Real Estate Index.

47. William Symonds, "College Crunch," *Business Week*, August 27, 2001.

48. Marilyn Chase, "Critics Chafe as More Doctors Offer Only Extra-Fee Concierge Care," *Wall Street Journal*, July 27, 2001.

49. Sylvester Scheiben and John Shoven first noted this problem in 1994. See "The Consequences of Population Aging on Private Pension Fund Saving and Asset Markets," Working Paper no. 4665 (Cambridge, Mass.: National Bureau of Economic Research, March 1994).

50. L. H. Summers and C. Carroll, "Why Is the U.S. Savings Rate So Low?" (Washington, D.C.: Brookings Papers on Economic Activity, 1987).

51. Suzanne Kapner, "Ford Chief to Resign: Chairman, An Heir, Is Successor," *New York Times*, October 30, 2001.

52. Johanna Berkman, "Harvard's Hoard," *New York Times Magazine*, June 24, 2001.

53. Laura Hruby and Elizabeth Schwinn, "Big Funds See a Dip in Assets," *Chronicle of Philanthropy* 13, no. 9 (2001).

54. Douglas V. Orr, "The Social Security Reform Debate: Effects of Institutional Changes in Labor and Financial Markets," Paper presented at the annual conference of the Allied Social Sciences Associations, Atlanta, Georgia, January 6, 2002.

55. Quoted in "How Jack Welch Runs GE," *Business Week*, May 28, 1998.

56. Institute for Policy Studies and United for a Fair Economy, *Executive Excess 2001* (Washington, D.C.: IPS, 2002).

57. Edward N. Wolff, *Top Heavy: The Increasing Inequality of Wealth in America and What Can Be Done about It* (New York: New Press, 2002).

58. Employee Benefit Research Council, cited in Beth Healy, "Battered Market Threatens Many Americans' Dreams," *Boston Globe*, July 14, 2002.

59. William Gross, Pinco Bond Fund, quoted in Harris Collingwood, "The Earnings Cult," *New York Times Magazine*, June 9, 2002.

60. "The Betrayed Investor," *Business Week*, February 25, 2002.

61. Paul Krugman, "Moles at Work," *New York Times*, October 11, 2002.

CHAPTER THREE

1. See David U. Himmelstein, Steffie Woolhandler, Ida Hellander, and Sidney M. Wolfe, "Quality of Care in Investor-Owned vs. Not-For-Profit HMOs," *Journal of the American Medical Association* 282, no. 2 (1999); and Steffie Woolhandler and David U. Himmelstein, "When Money Is the Mission—The High Costs of Investor-Owned Care," *New England Journal of Medicine* 341, no. 6 (1999).

2. Economists call a tax progressive when the rate of taxation—the amount of the tax relative to one's income—rises with income, as it does with the U.S. income tax. A regressive tax, on the other hand, levies a disproportionately high tax rate on those with lower incomes, as with a sales or excise tax.

3. For extensive collections of polling data with links to original sources, see www.pollingreport.com and "The Pulse: A Citizen's Guide to Public Opinion Data," at www.epinet.org/pulse.

4. Clyde Haberman, "NYC; Above 43d St., Every Second Still Counts," *New York Times*, November 11, 1997.

5. After deducting its own, fairly generous, operating expenses.

6. To be more precise, U.S. currency is liability on the balance sheet of the Federal Reserve, a topic discussed more thoroughly in chapter 4.

7. Keith Koffler, "Bush May Tap Retirement Funds to Avoid Hitting Debt Ceiling," *Government Executive Magazine*, March 12, 2002.

8. N. Gregory Mankiw, *Principles of Economics*, 2d ed. (Fort Worth, Tex.: Harcourt College Publishers, 2001), p. 571.

9. Although a study by Brookings Institute economist William Gale did find that *fears* of rising deficits in the future might cause interest rates to rise in the present.

10. Cited in Robert Eisner, *The Great Deficit Scares: The Federal Budget, Trade, and Social Security* (New York: Century Foundation, 1997), p 25.

11. James K. Galbraith, *Created Unequal: The Crisis in American Pay* (New York: Free Press, 1998), p. 191.

12. Tom Michl, "Debt, Deficits and the Distribution of Income," Discussion Paper no. 90-06 (Hamilton, N.Y.: Colgate University Department of Economics, July 1990).

13. "Address to the Nation on Federal Tax Reduction Legislation," quoted in Benjamin Friedman, *Day of Reckoning: The Consequences of American Economic Policy under Reagan and After* (New York: Random House, 1988), p. 236.

14. Thanks to loopholes and exemptions, few taxpayers actually paid the top 70 percent rate.

15. William Greider, "The Education of David Stockman," *Atlantic*, December 1981.

16. Paul Krugman, *The Age of Diminished Expectations: U.S. Economic Policy in the 1990s*, 3d ed. (Cambridge, Mass.: MIT Press, 1997).

17. Bob Woodward, *The Agenda: Inside the Clinton White House* (New York: Pocket Books, 1995).

18. For a thorough analysis of Clinton's economic policies see Robert Pollin, *Contours of Descent: U.S. Economic Fractures and the Landscape of Global Austerity* (London and New York: Verso, 2003).

19. David Firestone, "Conservatives Now See Deficits as a Tool to Fight Spending," *New York Times*, February 11, 2003.

20. The Center for Responsive Politics reports that financial firms contributed six times as much to Bush's 2000 presidential campaign as it did to Gore's.

21. The Bush administration's 2004 budget, for example, cut taxes sharply on the top 1 percent, increased military and security spending, but capped or cut funds for environmental protection, after-school programs, and early childhood education.

22. Interest rates in fact rose, thanks to actions of the Federal Reserve, a subject discussed in chapter 4.

23. James Brook, "Japan Battles Bond Rating," *New York Times*, July 6, 2002.

24. Margaret Popper, "Japanese-Style Woes in Germany," *Business Week*, August 5, 2002.

25. The subject of international finance and debt is discussed in detail in Chapter 5.

26. The $87,000 earnings cap is for 2003. This cap is adjusted each year for inflation.

27. Testimony of Michael Baroody, senior vice president for policy, communications, and public affairs, National Association of Manufacturers, on behalf of the Alliance for Worker Retirement Security, before the Republican National Committee Social Security Policy Briefing, June 19, 2000.

28. Alan Murray, "Clinton Plays to Aging Boomers," *Wall Street Journal*, March 29, 1999.

29. Milton Friedman, "Social Security Chimeras," *New York Times*, January 11, 1999.

30. President's Commission to Strengthen Social Security, *Strengthening Social Security and Creating Personal Wealth for Americans, Report of President's Commission* (Washington, D.C.: President's Commission to Strengthen Social Security, December 2001), p. 10.

31. Robert Borosage, "The Austerity Trap," *American Prospect*, September 24, 2001.

32. Robert Kuttner, "Tax and Spend," *American Prospect*, September 24, 2001.

33. Christopher Hitchens, *No One Left to Lie To: The Triangulations of William Jefferson Clinton* (London and New York: Verso, 1999).

34. Landowners, usually of the aristocracy, also captured a good share in the form of rents.

35. Those interested in an overview of economic debates in the 1800s and early 1900s might look at Robert L. Heilbroner, *The Worldly Philosophers: The Lives, Times, and Ideas of the Great Economic Thinkers*, rev. 7th ed. (New York: Simon and Schuster, 1999), and Daniel R. Fusfeld, *The Age of the Economist*, 9th ed. (Boston: Addison-Wesley, 2002).

36. George Lakoff, *Moral Politics: What Conservatives Know That Liberals Don't* (Chicago: University of Chicago Press, 1996).

37. Quoted in William Greider, "The Man From Alcoa," *Nation*, September 10, 2001.

38. Ibid.

39. See, for example, the comments of Benjamin Friedman, John

Shoven, Robert Barro, and James Tobin, in Henry Aaron and John Shoven, *Should the United States Privatize Social Security?* (Cambridge, Mass.: MIT Press, 1999).

40. John McKinnon, "Treasury Weighs Overhaul of Complete U.S. Tax Code," *Wall Street Journal*, October 30, 2002. Jonathan Weisman, "Inching Away from Income Tax Value-Added Levy Would Turn System Upside Down," *Washington Post*, October 31, 2002.

41. Phillip Shenon, "Hard Lobbying on Debtor Bill Pays Dividend," *New York Times*, March 13, 2001.

42. Rachel Emma Silverman, "The Retirement Welch Built Earns $1.4 Million a Month," *Wall Street Journal*, October 31, 2002.

43. Data based on author's analysis of Federal Reserve *Flow of Funds*. Additional data from Jane D'Arista, *Flow of Funds Review and Analysis*, Financial Markets Center, various issues. See also Lawrence Mishel, Jared Bernstein, and John Schmitt, *The State of Working America, 2000–2001* (Ithaca, N.Y.: Cornell University Press, 2001).

CHAPTER FOUR

1. Robert Shiller, "Why Do People Dislike Inflation?" in Christina D. Romer and David H. Romer, eds., *Reducing Inflation: Motivation and Strategy* (Chicago: University of Chicago Press, 1997).

2. A.W. Phillips, "The Relationship between Unemployment and the Rate of Change in Money Wages in the United Kingdom, 1861–1957," *Economica* 25, no. 2 (November 1958).

3. Kenneth McLaughlin, "Rigid Wages?" *Journal of Monetary Economics* 34 (1994).

4. Michael Bruno, "Does Inflation Really Lower Growth?" *Finance and Development*, September 1995.

5. Justin Wolfers, "Is Business Cycle Volatility Costly? Evidence from Surveys of Subjective Well-being," Working Paper no. 9619 (Cambridge, Mass.: National Bureau of Economic Research, April 2003).

6. Edward Wolff, "The Distributional Effects of the 1969–1975 Inflation on Holdings of Household Wealth in the United States,"

Review of Income and Wealth 25 (1979); see also Edward Wolff, *Top Heavy: A Study of the Increasing Inequality of Wealth in America* (New York: Twentieth Century Fund, 1995).

7. Milton Friedman, "Using Escalators to Fight Inflation," *Fortune*, July 1974.

8. F. A. Hayek, "Choice in Currency: A Way to Stop Inflation," Occasional Paper no. 48 (London: Institute of Economic Affairs, 1976).

9. The argument that inflation results from distributional conflicts in a society was first formalized by Bob Rowthorn; see Rowthorn, "Conflict, Inflation and Money," *Cambridge Journal of Economics* 1 (1977), and Rowthorn and Andrew Glyn, "The Diversity of Unemployment Experience Since 1973," in Stephen A. Marglin and Juliet B. Schor, eds., *The Golden Age of Capitalism: Reinterpreting the Postwar Experience* (Oxford and New York: Oxford University Press, 1990). See also William Vickrey, *Metastatics and Macroeconomics* (New York: Harcourt, Brace, and World, 1964).

10. Data cited in Robert Pollin, with Elizabeth Zahrt, "Expansionary Policy for Full Employment in the United States: Retrospective on the 1960s and Current Period Prospects," in Jonathan Michie and John Grieve Smith, eds., *Employment and Economic Performance: Jobs, Inflation and Growth* (Oxford and New York: Oxford University Press, 1997), pp. 36–75.

11. Robert Solow, "The Intelligent Citizen's Guide to Inflation," *Public Interest*, winter 1975.

12. William Fellner, "Towards a Reconstruction of Macroeconomics" (Washington, D.C.: American Enterprise Institute, 1976).

13. William Greider, *Secrets of the Temple: How the Federal Reserve Runs the Country* (New York: Simon and Schuster, 1987), pp. 482–83.

14. Bob Woodward, *Maestro: Greenspan's Fed and the American Boom* (New York: Simon and Schuster, 2000), pp. 62 and 90.

15. James Galbraith, "The Surrender of Economic Policy," *American Prospect* 7, no. 25.

16. Dean Baker and Jared Bernstein, "Full Employment: Don't Give It Up without a Fight," Working Paper no. 122 (Washington, D.C.: Economic Policy Institute, January 2002).

17. Woodward, *Maestro*, p. 168.
18. Quoted in Robert Pollin, "Wage Bargaining and the U.S. Phillip's Curve: Was Greenspan Right about the Traumatized Worker in the 1990s?" Paper presented at the annual meeting of the Allied Social Science Association, Washington, D.C., January 2003.
19. Paul Krugman. "Is the Maestro a Hack?" *New York Times*, February 7, 2003, and "On the Second Day, Atlas Waffled," *New York Times*, February 14, 2003.
20. For detailed analysis of the political loyalties and pressures on the Federal Reserve, See Gerald Epstein and Thomas Ferguson, "Monetary Policy, Loan Liquidation, and Industrial Conflict," in Thomas Ferguson, *Golden Rule: The Investment Theory of Party Competition and the Logic of Money Driven Political Systems* (Chicago: University of Chicago Press, 1995), and Gerald Epstein, "Domestic Stagflation and Monetary Policy," in Thomas Ferguson, *The Hidden Election: Politics and Economics in the 1980 Presidential Campaign* (New York: Pantheon Books, 1981).
21. See chapter six for a more detailed discussion of currency boards.
22. This is not to say that downturns are caused by restrictive monetary policy. Although this has often been the case, history is replete with investment booms and busts that flame up and burn out of their own accord.
23. Federal Reserve Board, *Survey of Consumer Finances*.
24. Willem Thorbecke, "Disinflationary Monetary Policy and the Distribution of Income," Working Paper no. 185 (Annandale-on-Hudson, N.Y.: Jerome Levy Economics Institute, March 1997).
25. This account draws upon various works of the economists Randall Wray, University of Missouri at Kansas City, Robert Pollin, University of Massachusetts and the Political Economy Research Institute, and Edwin Dickens, Drew University.
26. William Vickrey, "Fifteen Fatal Fallacies of Financial Fundamentalism," in Aaron W. Warner, Mathew Forstater, and Sumner M. Rosen, eds., *Commitment to Full Employment: The Economics and Social Policy of William Vickrey* (Armonk, N.Y.: M. E. Sharpe, 2000).
27. David Stires, "The Breaking Point," *Fortune*, March 3, 2003.

28. Gerald Epstein and Juliet Schor, "Macropolicy in the Rise and Fall of the Golden Age," in Marglin and Schor, eds., *The Golden Age of Capitalism*, and "The Divorce of the Banca D'Italia and the Italian Treasury: A Case Study of Central Bank Independence," in Peter Lange and Marino Regini, eds., *State, Market and Social Regulation: New Perspectives on Italy* (Cambridge and New York: Cambridge University Press, 1989).

29. Andrew Glyn, "Labor Market Deregulation and European Unemployment," Paper presented at the annual meeting of the Allied Social Science Association, Washington, D.C., January 2003.

30. Dimitri Papadimitriou, "Full Employment Policy," in Warner, et al., *Commitment to Full Employment: The Economics and Social Policy of William S. Vickrey* (Armonk, N.Y.: M. E. Sharpe, 2000).

31. Robert Pollin, with E. Zahrt, "Expansionary Policy."

32. Robert Pollin, *URPE (Union for Radical Political Economics) Newsletter*, winter 2003.

33. Reuters, "Producer Prices Rise 1.6% to Thirteen Year High," February 20, 2003.

CHAPTER FIVE

1. The G7, or Group of Seven, consists of Britain, Canada, France, Germany, Italy, Japan, and the United States. G-7 economic ministers meet annually to discuss global economic problems. When geopolitical concerns are on the agenda, the group is expanded to eight (the G-8), which includes Russia.

2. Data on international debt can be found at the Web site of the World Bank, www.worldbank.org.

3. Cheryl Payer, *The Debt Trap* (New York: Monthly Review Press, 1974).

4. For an excellent overview and critique of IMF policy, see Joseph Stiglitz, *Globalization and Its Discontents* (New York: W. W. Norton, 2002).

5. Quoted in Joseph Kahn, "Treasury Secretary Offers a New Vision for the IMF," *New York Times*, December 15, 1999.

6. Thomas L. Friedman, *The Lexus and the Olive Tree* (New York: Farrar, Straus, Giroux, 1999).

7. Barbara Garson, *Money Makes the World Go Around* (New York: Viking Press, 2001).

8. Say a pound of beef costs 2 real to produce in Brazil and 2 dollars to produce in the United States. At a one-to-one exchange rate, Brazilian producers can sell beef in America at a competitive price. If one year later prices have risen 10 percent in Brazil but remained stable in the United States, then Brazilian beef will now cost 2.2 reals while U.S. beef costs 2 dollars. At a one-to-one exchange rate, U.S. importers need 2 dollars to buy 2 real, but the 2 real are no longer sufficient to pay for a pound of Brazilian beef. Brazilian beef exports will suffer unless the real is devalued by 10 percent to equalize foreign and domestic prices.

9. Larry Rohter, "Brazil's Leader Angers His Old Allies," *New York Times*, March 22, 2003.

10. International Monetary Fund, Seminar on Capital Account Liberalization, Press Conference, March 10, 1998, http://www.imf.org/external/np/tr/1998/tr980310.htm.

11. Paul Blustein, "Bankruptcy System for Nations Fails to Draw Support," *Washington Post*, April 2, 2003.

12. Michel Chossudovsky, *Globalisation of Poverty: the Impacts of IMF and World Bank Reforms* (London: Pluto Press, 2000).

13. Joseph Stiglitz, *Globalization and Its Discontents.*

14. Kate Bronfenbrenner, "We'll Close! Plant Closings, Plant Closing Threats, Union Organizing, and NAFTA," *Multinational Monitor* 18 (1997).

15. A point made even by the arch-conservative *Economist* magazine, in an editorial titled "A Place for Capital Controls," May 1, 2003.

16. Peter Temin, *Lessons from the Great Depression* (Cambridge, Mass.: MIT Press, 1991).

CHAPTER SIX

1. World Council of Churches, press release, May 9, 2003, www.wcc-coe.org.

2. Quoted in David Crane, "America No Longer a Model for a Decent Society," *Toronto Star*, May 3, 2003.

3. Michael Mandel, "Class Warfare?" *Business Week*, January 20, 2003.

4. For an extensive survey of these "wealth broadening" policy ideas, see "Homestead Security: Broadening America's Riches," *American Prospect*, May 2003.

5. Jim Yardley, "Well-Off but Still Pressed, Doctor Could Use Tax Cut," *New York Times*, April 7, 2001.

6. Quoted in Elisabeth Bumiller, "Cheney Returns Fire in Battle on Tax Cuts," *New York Times*, January 11, 2003.

7. Milton Friedman, "What Every American Wants," *Wall Street Journal*, January 15, 2003.

8. Quoted in John Tierney, "Republicans Explain an About-Face," *New York Times*, May 24, 2003.

9. Quoted in Robert Dreyfuss, "Grover Norquist: 'Field Marshall' of the Bush Plan," *Nation*, May 14, 2001.

ACKNOWLEDGMENTS

Many thanks to the friends, colleagues, and relatives whose insights, efforts, and advice made this book possible. Marty Wolfson, Jane D'Arista, Don Goldstein, Doug Orr, Tom Palley, and Carroll Estes provided thoughtful critical comments on some of my early attempts to nail these ideas down in technical papers. Ann Wetherilt, Helen Ahearn, and Elaine Schear offered much-needed moral support and writing advice. Bob Pollin, Bob Tierney, and Rich Rosen read early drafts, and their comments were invaluable in clarifying the content and prose. Emmanuel College's generous financial support paid for, among other things, diligent and good-humored research assistance from Rebecca Frade. Amy Caldwell at Beacon Press pulled everything together into a readable book. My husband, Victor, read multiple drafts, listened to me think out loud, put up with me, and remained a loving partner and friend.

Above all, I want to thank and acknowledge the hundreds of smart, dedicated, and socially concerned economists in the International Confederation of Associations for Pluralism in Economics (ICAPE) and affiliated schools and organizations who taught and inspired me.

INDEX

expansionary monetary policy,
133–34
export-import loans, 89
exports, 103, 156, 160–61, 165,
171, 183–84

FAC (Federal Advisory Council),
132
Faux, Jeff, 35–36, 139
Federal Advisory Council (FAC),
132
federal budget: balanced federal
budget, 12, 75, 76, 84, 85,
87, 91, 192; deficits in, 68,
72–93; "full-employment
budgeting," 75, 85; from
1930s to 1998, 75–76, 83;
surpluses in, 7, 76, 85, 86, 87,
103. *See also* debt, national;
deficit spending
federal debt. *See* debt, national
Federal Open Market Committee
(FOMC), 132
Federal Reserve: and bailout of
Mexico, 162; board of, 132;
and Congress, 131, 134–35,
136, 150; definition of,
114; district banks, 131,
Greenspan as chair of, 19,
136–42, 148; and inflation,
6–7, 16, 113, 115, 123, 130,
136–42; and interest rates,
6–7, 78, 130, 132, 135, 136,
139, 142, 147; mass media on,
141–42; monetary policy of,
133–34; and money supply,
68, 70, 130, 135, 154; origins
of, 131; power of, 17; and price

stability, 141; regulation of
returns on bonds and bank
accounts by, 10; and statistics
on net sales of equities, 52;
structure of, 131–32; Volcker
as chair of, 129–30, 134–36,
141, 143–44; wealth distribution surveys by, 2, 22, 146
Federal Reserve Act (1913), 131
Fed Funds rate, 114, 133, 136,
140, 141, 147
finance industry: and consumer
bankruptcy, 108; and con-
sumption taxes, 108; and
crowding-out myth, 88; and
definition of investment, 107;
and European deficit spending, 92–93; and Federal
Reserve, 132; and inflation,
119–21, 122, 129; and
Japanese securities, 92, 93;
output of and employment in,
12, 14; and privatization of
Social Security, 107–8; public
image of, 21; and rentiers,
119–21, 122, 129, 145; and
Republican Party, 89
financial advisers, 46, 47–48,
49, 62
financial rhetoric. *See* economic
rhetoric
financial speculation, 135, 136,
148, 176
fiscal stabilization policy, 71–72
FOMC (Federal Open Market
Committee), 132
food stamps, 74, 83, 89
Forbes 400, 23, 28